Fund-Raising for Higher Education

FUND-RAISING FOR HIGHER EDUCATION

by JOHN A. POLLARD

Vice-President,
Council for Financial Aid to Education

FOREWORD BY Frank W. Abrams

HARPER & BROTHERS, PUBLISHERS
NEW YORK

Library of Congress catalog card number: 58–11052

With admiration and respect,
this book is dedicated to
FRANK W. ABRAMS
IRVING S. OLDS
WALTER P. PAEPCKE
HENNING W. PRENTIS, JR.
ALFRED P. SLOAN, JR.
From its beginnings in 1636, American
higher education has had no better
friends than they.

Contents

Foreword

FRANK W. ABRAMS
*Former Chairman of the Board,
Standard Oil Company (New Jersey)*

It seemed refreshing to me as a friend of education to read the manuscript of a book on the financial needs of our colleges and our ways of meeting these needs, without the awesome threat of Sputnik as the motivating cause for action. But then, anyone who really knows the author, John Pollard, can understand that the "ways and means" proposed therein are based on a long experience with the problems of financing higher education and on a personal dedication to their solution.

Someone has said that each time the people of a democracy meet a great national crisis successfully they lose some part of their personal freedoms in the process. And, of course, we face another situation of this kind with the near-hysteria that has accompanied the recent indications of the scientific progress of the Russians. They have gained mightily by compulsion, while we have lost position through neglect of the voluntary process.

Dr. Pollard's book, without design for the purpose, points the way for the democratic means of achieving our educational defense without surrendering to the urge of looking to Washington. The present situation doubtless requires Federal attention, but the extent and permanence of it can be limited by our willingness to act in our private, independent capacity. This book, for that purpose, is a call to arms.

ACKNOWLEDGMENTS

This book is a small illustration of a big *mot* of Dr. Samuel Johnson: "Knowledge is of two kinds: we know a subject ourselves, or we know where we can find information upon it." The conception of the book (November 1952) was in one mind; its execution is the product of many. Since October 1953, the originator has been the happy (and complete) servant of a "new idea" in American society, the Council for Financial Aid to Education.

How to complete a book designed in high hope—as the council was—to aid America's colleges and universities would have been an insoluble problem except for the eager interest and the willingness of many people to contribute their expert information to what in truth is a joint project. They are named here, in grateful acknowledgment, along with Ordway Tead, an editor whose long recognized ability is equalled by his patience.

Frank W. Abrams	Austin V. McClain
David M. Church	Clarence J. Myers
Frieda Creutzmann	Kriz Planka
Arnaud C. Marts	Harold J. Seymour
Ernest T. Stewart, Jr.	

Amherst College	Carleton College
J. Alfred Guest	Robert L. Gale
California Institute of	Colby College
Technology	A. G. Eustis
Charles Newton	Edward H. Turner

Cornell University
  F. Weston Prior
  J. L. Zwingle
Dartmouth College
  George H. Colton
  Nichol M. Sandoe, Jr.
  Ford H. Whelden
Harvard University
  David McCord
Hastings College
  Dale D. Welch
Lehigh University
  Paul J. Franz, Jr.
Northwestern University
  Lynford E. Kautz
Occidental College
  Lyman Thompson
  Joseph H. Wadsworth
Ohio State University
  Kenyon S. Campbell
Princeton University
  George J. Cooke, Jr.
  Edgar M. Gemmell

Rensselaer Polytechnic
  Institute
  Richard W. Schmelzer
Stanford University
  David S. Jacobson
Swarthmore College
  Joseph B. Shane
United Negro College Fund
  William J. Trent, Jr.
University of Denver
  George N. Rainsford
University of Notre Dame
  James E. Armstrong
University of Pennsylvania
  Chester E. Tucker
Vassar College
  Helen H. Couch
Wellesley College
  Elinor Anderson
Yale University
  Charles M. O'Hearn
  Charles Watson, 3rd

My final acknowledgment of aid is to the Council for Financial Aid to Education. By arrangement with the chairman of its executive committee, I was able to devote a three-day weekend during the last four months of 1957 to the completion of this book.

One word about the Council for Financial Aid to Education. Its objective is to help increase the financial support and understanding of all branches of American higher education. Under its charter the Council is prohibited from soliciting, accepting, or disbursing money.

Because of the very small numbers of its staff, the Council necessarily has concentrated on trying to help more *donors*—large business concerns especially—to develop aid-to-education programs. In spite of many requests, it has not been possible for the CFAE staff to work with *recipient* colleges and universities on their development programs.

This book, it is hoped, may be helpful to the colleges. It makes no pretense of giving "all the answers." Every college must find these for itself, in the light of its own special problems. Yet this book does give practical information, grounded in the experience of many colleges and universities, which may be of general use in meeting these problems.

Today American higher education faces a job of great magnitude. Careful and exhaustive studies, state by state, have shown the bulging enrollments which will descend upon our colleges and universities between 1958 and 1970. Many institutions will then face a double problem: 1) how to make up some deficiencies in the financial structure and in plant and equipment which date from World War II years, and 2) how to acquire the further expanded financial resources which they will require during the next several decades in order to meet obligations to their constituencies and to the nation.

Many well informed individuals and educational organizations have considered the problem. All grasp its size. All agree that the 1,800 to 1,900 colleges, universities, professional and technological schools, and two-year colleges in the United States will have to work out the problem each in its own way. But one fact is binding upon all of them. They must plan in detail for the future, put still greater emphasis on quality of educational programs and performance, think in large terms of their responsibilities, and then make sound forward plans to procure adequate financing. The nation is able to provide it. The colleges will have to make a convincing case for it.

Mr. Alfred P. Sloan, Jr., in two talks before educational and business groups in 1955, underscored the necessity for long-range development plans among the colleges and universities. Soundly managed business concerns, he pointed out, always have the forward look. Their executives have a vision of what and where they would like to have the companies be, say, ten to twenty years hence. Mr. Sloan, a warm friend and supporter of higher education and a trustee of Massachusetts Institute of Technology, believes that presidents and trustees of our colleges and universities have a similar responsibility: to lead, not to drift; to think large, and in terms rather of opportunity than of need; and to remember that the people of the United States like high quality and will support a quality performance with ample means.

This same attitude was expressed in 1907 by Daniel Burnham, famous Chicago architect and city planner. He said:

> Make no little plans; they have no magic to stir men's blood and probably themselves will not be realized. Make big plans; aim high in hope and work, remembering that a noble, logical diagram once recorded will never die, but long after we are gone will be a living thing, asserting itself with ever-growing insistency. Remember that our sons and grandsons are going to do things that would stagger us. Let your watchword be order and your beacon beauty. Think big.*

Higher education in the United States has become big—a "growth industry." It is fast becoming bigger, in response to the nation's demand for unprecedentedly larger numbers of educated men and women in nearly all walks of life. Patently the nation is well able to afford the big underwriting required by the college-university enterprise.

The book is designed to aid colleges and universities in their *constituency relations*. It endeavors to identify the various constituencies of United States colleges and universities, and to set forth ways and means used to cultivate them. It represents educational fund-raising as, in fact, it is: a regular and continuing administrative function, best managed through a development program, or "continuous campaign."

---

* Charles Moore, *Daniel H. Burnham, Architect, Planner of Cities* (Boston and New York: Houghton Mifflin Company, 1921), Vol II, p. 147.

Gifts from all possible sources, both to capital and to income, have to be sought continuously so that the college can develop steadily. A well organized and directed development program, with competent personnel giving constant attention and spark to the machinery, is today an inescapable necessity for a college or university. Every one must plan its growth, realistically and systematically. No college can afford not to have a development program.

The potential support available to American colleges and universities is indicated by the following statistics.

In its report entitled *Higher Education in a Decade of Decision*, published in 1957, the Educational Policies Commission of the National Education Association showed that total expenditures for higher education in the United States rose from $503 million in 1929–1930 to $2,821 million in 1953–1954. During this period the gross national product increased from $91,105 million to $360,654 million and higher education's share of the gross national product from 0.55 per cent to 0.78 per cent—approximately 0.01 per cent annually.

The Educational Policies Commission made three projections of future funds for higher education, on the basis of Federal Government estimates of growth in the gross national product: to $436 billion in 1960, to $525 billion in 1965, and to $634 billion in 1975. The Commission decided that, barring depression or war, its second projection was the most realistic of the three: that in the period 1955–1975 higher education would receive 0.01 per cent a year more of the gross national product, the average yearly gain of the last twenty-five years. Thus higher education's share of the estimated gross national product of $634 billion in 1975 should be 0.99 per cent, or $6,283 million. This amount would be more than double the 1954 expenditures for higher education.

These figures do not represent a flight into unknown space. Using Federal Government reports, The American Association of Fund-Raising Counsel estimated that voluntary gifts and grants to United States colleges and universities in the period 1939–1940 to 1953–1954 totaled $2,409,383,048. The rate of growth was as follows:

	1939–40	1953–54	Increase
Number of institutions	1,708	1,871	
Resident enrollment	1,494,203	2,514,712	68%
Private gifts and grants for current purposes	$40,453,000	$191,259,000	373%
Gifts for endowment	$41,169,000	$100,114,000	143%
Gifts for plant expansion	$22,664,000	$103,900,000	358%
Value of plant and plant funds	$2,303,302,488	$7,559,556,000	228%
Value of endowments	$1,686,282,767	$3,196,120,000	90%

A survey of voluntary giving to higher education in the fiscal year 1954–1955, made by the Council for Financial Aid to Education and the American College Public Relations Association, showed total receipts of between $507 million and $514 million. During the fiscal year 1957–1958 this total may approach $700 million.

Meanwhile, legislative appropriations for tax-supported colleges and universities—Federal, state, and municipal—also have been rising. During 1956–1957 the total expenditures of our higher educational institutions were about $3,250 million.

In brief, the American people now perceive the importance of higher education to the nation. They will provide ampler financial support. This almost surely will go to the colleges and universities which have defined their roles and are planning their development with the most skill. Like mercy, philanthropy blesses both the giver and the receiver. But American philanthropy for higher education in the foreseeable future is likely to fall chiefly where there has been the most careful "seeding."

This book, while based on the broad concept of *constituency relations,* undertakes to show the main elements of the development program and how it is best organized and made to work. The best fund-raising experience of American colleges and universities, extending over three centuries, has been sifted for tried and proved principles which may be applied to insuring the growth of our colleges and universities today.

At the outset it will be well to consider a few of these basic principles.

January 1958   J. A. P.

1. The first principle of fund-raising for any college or university is that it should carry on a sound educational program. Tinsel does not attract gold.

2. A belief in the quality of an institution, and in the importance of what it is doing, is the main motive for contributing to it.

3. A college or university having a first-rank function to perform for society should never cease hunting for—and striving to merit—the money which it needs from society in order to give it the best possible service.

4. Askings should be held down to legitimate needs for growth and development. It is as unwise to seek too much as too little.

5. Raising funds for a college or university is radically important work, vital to the work of the classroom and laboratory which it helps to make possible.

6. It is a four-season, round-the-clock job.

7. It is professional work, a task for a competent director on full time and in full charge.

8. Trying to muddle through on a "spare part" or "spare time" basis always proves to be expensive economy.

9. There is nothing about the work of fund-raising which a permanent member or members of the college administrative staff can not master. It requires more perspiration than inspiration, though both are useful.

10. The work of raising funds is not beneath the dignity of a president, but should not be solely his responsibility.

11. It is the business of everybody who has a stake in the institution—trustees, president, alumni, other friends, parents of students, business and industry, and civic groups.

12. That college is best circumstanced which has the largest body of devoted friends, under strong leadership, working regularly and in an organized way in its behalf.

13. The only way to raise money is to ask for it; and the more people there are asking in behalf of a college, the better.

14. In its relations with these volunteers or enlistees, a college is wise to remember the virtue of giving as well as the necessity of getting.

15. Every approach to every member of a college's constituency should be pitched on the level of important business.

16. All possible sources of support for a college or university must be exploited regularly and thoroughly. The wise institution will conduct its financial campaign continuously and on the broadest scale possible—the annual fund, the bequest program, the search for memorial funds, for grants for research, for capital gifts for specific endowments and buildings, and for gifts from business corporations.

17. Good public relations is an indispensable aid to raising funds, but not a means. Before asking for money the institution has to explain its work skillfully to its constituency, which can never be too well informed. Samuel Johnson said, "A man, sir, must keep his friendship in constant repair." So with an institution.

18. An intensive campaign for capital gifts, at intervals, is an almost inescapable necessity. But a high-pressure campaign is only a *temporary* part of an institution's whole financial problem, which is a *permanent* fact.

19. The development program, embodying the principles of the continuous campaign, is the sound, long-term plan.

20. Fund-raising for a college or university is a regular and continuing administrative function. It must be directed by a competent person giving full time to it. In order to get best results from it, he must make it an effective team operation.

Fund-Raising for
Higher Education

I

The Bedrock of Good Public Relations

Mere publicity is like reputation—what you are thought to be; but real public relations is like character—what you really are. Public relations is deeds, not words.

—CLARENCE A. SCHOENFELD

It is an excellent thing to enjoy a good character. A man can hardly get on without the asset of goodwill which it attracts, and an institution not at all. To be on good terms with one's fellows and to have their confidence and respect is indispensable to a man's career, and equally to the growth and development of social institutions. Imperatively an institution has to be known favorably to its various constituencies.

This truism takes on double force when a college or university—or any other social institution—has to seek new financial resources to buttress its work. For all appeals for funds have to be solidly based on the bedrock of good public relations. That is the "kick off" point for all fund-raising appeals. It is also the terminal point of any effective appeal, by which it should be further strengthened.

All successful fund-raising begins with good public relations. In essence this term embraces every appropriate means by which an institution can maintain a good footing with its publics. "PR" is a subtle and varied instrument of policy, likely in unskilled hands to cut the wrong way, and employed with best results only when it is managed with intelligence and resourcefulness. Public relations goes far beyond publicity, or

1

hanging the name up in public where it can be seen by all. The mere appearance of a college's name in print is, by itself, neither important nor fruitful.

A practitioner has given the essence of the public relations task for American education:

1. Improved public relations is needed as never before if our schools are to continue to merit and receive adequate support.

2. Public relations correctly conceived is no bag of publicity tricks; it is inextricably linked with sound administration in all its aspects.

3. Public relations is not the job of a single individual; every contact between the university and its constituency is an episode in the complex flow of institutional relationships.[1]

Public relations, in short, is a comprehensive program deliberately conceived to convey a total impression of the quality of the institution which it represents to the public. Its end is to maintain goodwill and enhance prestige.

These assets are hard won, and if an institution has wisdom, it treasures and nurtures them carefully. A college or university has need of them always, and never so critically as when it is required to lay before its constituencies a case for fresh financial support.

That is why merit alone, nothing else, makes it possible for a college or university to win prestige and goodwill. Woodrow Wilson perceived this when he said: "The reputation of a university is not a matter of report. It is a matter of fact." [2]

Because, in the eyes of their constituencies, their reputations stem from excellent performance of the functions that institutions of higher education should rightly assume, three of our most highly regarded universities have, at different times, raised millions of dollars by appeals based on simple, direct statements of fact:

"Cornell—Greater Still—By Your Will."

"An Investment for All Time." (Northwestern.)

"For a Finer, Not a Bigger, Yale."

These three institutions and others have been able to enlist support adequate to their purposes because they keep their houses in good order. That part of public relations which consists of telling the institution's story effectively is, when the story is based on sound values, fairly easy. President Eliot gave Harvard a rebirth by his insistence on excellence and by his skill in selecting outstanding men and giving them important work to do.

By any careful test the substance of good public relations is the solid achievements of an institution's faculty, alumni, and students; or significant new steps in education which the college or university takes because it has the men (or women) qualified to make them of special value. Involved here are what President E. B. Fred of the University of Wisconsin calls "the three C's of higher education: a *community* of scholars with *creative* ability and great *curiosity*." [3] The various segments which make up an institution's constituency can nearly always be depended upon to discriminate between sound and legitimate work on the one hand, and showy experiments on the other.

It bears repeating: excellence has to be the standard for the whole of a college or university, and when this standard is attained in any high degree, public relations is no problem.

These are general considerations of policy,* but they are of basic importance to the ultimate objective—effective fund-

* The main concern here is not with the techniques of public relations, but with the good effects on fund-raising of a sound program. The American College Public Relations Association freely exchanges ideas and techniques through its *ACPRA News Letter* and its journal *Pride*. There are also numerous books on the subject, including Clarence A. Schoenfeld's excellent *The University and Its Publics*. (New York: Harper & Brothers, 1954.) In *The American College*, edited by P. F. Valentine (New York: Philosophical Library, 1949), there is a useful chapter on public relations written by W. Emerson Reck, now Vice President of Wittenberg College.

raising for higher education. How, it is fair to ask, do these considerations apply to the management of an institution's public relations program so that it will facilitate the raising of money?

Limited Constituency

First of all, the immediate constituency of a college or university is limited in size, but select and more than ordinarily discriminating. Dr. John D. Millett, now President of Miami University, has pointed out that only half of the people in the United States have gone beyond grade school and less than 10 per cent of our adult population are college graduates.[4] The public relations program directed to this logical but small group of constituents cannot, if it is to be fruitful in results, be based on the techniques of mass appeal. Taste and selectiveness must be the principal guides.

Beauty queens and all-conquering athletic teams may attract a glitter to some eyes, but they do not, as the total experience of our most esteemed colleges and universities makes clear, serve as the magnet for money.

The Virtue of Giving

A second important fact stems from the first. Since the main constituency of a college or university is not large, it can and should be invited in to see the institution at work. Public relations, wisely conceived, does much more than merely tell the constituency by means of newspaper releases, radio programs, bulletins and other publications, and speeches. It also invites the constituency to come and see typical and important things that the institution is doing—in classroom, laboratory, theater, special forums or institutes, and even in the homes of the president and members of the faculty. American Education Week in the autumn is a logical time for such visitations. Students can be brought into effective participation in all affairs of this kind.

Some of our older private colleges and universities, out of a distillation of long experience, have learned to place a high value on this sort of "family relationship" with their constituents. Annually since 1914 Yale has held open house on Alumni University Day, February 22, and it is heartening to see the quality of the graduates who return for the occasion, and the serious interest which they take in the University's work. Princeton has a similar custom.

These and numerous other colleges and universities know that this kind of relationship, grounded in warm mutual interest, is appreciated by the alumni and invaluable to the institution. As a matter of policy it is wise for a college or university, in its relations with its constituencies, to keep in mind the virtue of giving as well as the necessity of getting.

The President's Role

Closely related, a third cardinal point of public relations policy is that the president, no matter how numerous the roles he has to fill in a taxing job, must above all represent the institution of which he is the chief executive officer. He is officially its head, generally its spokesman, and inevitably its delegate. By the nature of his office he is the main link and symbol between college and constituency. A. Lawrence Lowell stated the fact nicely: "But the president, though not in a position of command, must be the leader if he has a pattern to carry out." [5]

Like an orchestra conductor, he has to lead, to bring harmony out of the various people and groups whose best efforts he must try to evoke—in the president's case, the faculty, trustees, alumni, students, parents, and other interested friends among the public at large. What he has to create is an educational program which will have the firm support of the faculty and the trustees, and which he can make articulate to the constituencies from which he has to enlist support.

Qualifications of the "PR" Director

A fourth principle of public relations policy is manifest. The "PR" director should be heard in the administrative council of the college or university, for which he can oftentimes save prestige, goodwill, and dollars. C. A. Schoenfeld gives the reason: "True public relations . . . is primarily a matter of policy. Consequently the man charged with the PR assignment must be brought into the inner circles, at least unofficially." [6]

For this assignment a college or university should employ only a person of stature whose understanding of its functions can win the trust of the campus community, and whose grasp of the media of communications will enable him to deal effectively on its behalf with the public. The right man for the job will, like Janus, look in both directions.

He must have a sense of what is choice and excellent, of what is most important among the varied activities of the institution that he represents, and of taste and integrity in all that he does relating to its constituencies. He is an interpreter working in a two-way communications system.

Periodic Reporting

This fact points to a fifth cardinal principle of educational public relations. A college or university, since it seeks financial support from its publics, is obliged to make a periodic accounting to them of the way in which it has used the funds received. Most of the tax-supported universities publish annual financial reports, and some are required by law to do so. In contrast, many of the privately supported colleges and universities hold to the attitude that their treasurer's reports are of concern only to the president, the trustees, and the faculty. This view is myopic. It is one reason why the opinion lingers, especially among many businessmen, that colleges and universities do not manage their financial affairs as well as they should.

The more enlightened view on financial reporting is held by the heads of the oldest general-welfare foundations. Such foundations originate in private benefactions, but are incorporated under public laws. And as the heads of the Carnegie Corporation of New York and the Rockefeller Foundation began saying many years ago, foundations are obliged, in their own and in the public interest, to make a public accounting of their management of the funds which they hold in trust for the welfare of mankind.

This positive attitude is, fortunately, winning greater acceptance among institutions of higher education. In the foreword to a recent study, the National Federation of College and University Business Officers Associations said:

The data can be of great help in assuring those who provide financial support that institutions' funds are being used wisely and well to uphold standards of excellence of academic programs. Without such data, donors must take on faith the soundness of the allocation of funds to the many activities of the institutions, and the skill and diligence of those administering their budgets. There is a growing interest among donors in a demonstration of budgetary soundness, skill, and diligence.[7]

This Federation and the American Council on Education have urged every college and university to publish an annual financial report. How widely the report will be distributed is for each college or university to decide. In the view of the American Council on Education, however, it "should be as wide as possible in order that representatives of the public and members of the groups responsible for the support of the institution may be adequately informed of its financial affairs."[8]

In that enlightened spirit, Fenn College ("a Cleveland institution dedicated to serving the Cleveland community") published its Annual Report for 1954–1955 in the *Cleveland Plain Dealer* on November 16, 1955. Explaining this unusual action, President G. Brooks Earnest wrote:

Today, the operation of a college or university is big business. And like most businesses, a college is primarily concerned with improving the quality and performance of its product (the students) through the increased skill of its personnel (the faculty), production techniques (educational processes), and plant improvements and expansion (classrooms and laboratories).

Annually, most business firms submit a report of the previous year's operation to the stockholders. At Fenn, we have no stockholders as such since we are a corporation not-for-profit under the laws of the State of Ohio. However, we feel that the people of Greater Cleveland, who have shared in our many educational dividends since our founding, all own stock in the College. And as stockholders, we know you will be interested in this report on our operation for the year 1954–55.

Subsequently other colleges—notably Mills, in Oakland, California—have followed Fenn's example and used their local newspapers to make public financial reports. Results are reported to be favorable.

Attractive and informative financial reports are published also by Harvard, the University of Illinois, Massachusetts Institute of Technology, Rutgers, Washington University, and Wesleyan University, to name but a few.

Printing for Promotion

Within reasonable budgetary limits, a college or university should buy the best printing it can procure. Especially, the best thought should go into the editing of the bulletin or catalogue of courses, and the best taste into its production. This bulletin should, in a word, be recognized as important and given careful consideration by responsible members of the faculty and administrative staff.[9] The bulletin is always a historical record; sometimes it is a promotional piece as well.

Bard College during 1956 broke new ground with a publication entitled "Where Do We Go from Here?" The objective was not to do away with the catalogue but to develop an inexpensive publication that would help a student to decide whether or not he wanted to go to Bard. Faculty, administration, and students worked together and devised a pertly illustrated sixteen-page publication which 1) described the kind of college Bard is and the kind of student it is interested in attracting, and 2) was inexpensive. Bard catalogues used to cost 25 cents apiece, and view books 20 cents.

"Where Do We Go from Here?" in humorous fashion put a series of illustrated questions to prospective matriculants:

Are you?
venturesome
inquisitive
discriminating
enthusiastic
independent
perceptive
(and, of course) original

A brief description of the Bard program, also in question form, rounded out the publication. The finished product cost 2½ cents to print. It proved so popular and effective that, since the initial mailing, the college has received requests for more than 10,000 additional copies.

Any college's or university's bulletin of courses or educational program ought to be its best presentation piece—accurate and precise in content, well designed and illustrated, and tastefully printed. Yet probably four-fifths of our institutions of higher education do their printing "on the cheap," and it is expensive economy. A wise observer touched his finger to the heart of the matter: "When you go calling on the public, carry a graphic bouquet. Ink and fine paper assure the pleasure of your company." *

* *Direct Advertising*, in two issues—fourth quarter 1952 and first quarter 1953—published a perceptive article by Claire Imrie, "Alma Mater, You Hold Your Head High, But Your Slip Is Showing in Most of Your Printing." It is instructive and helpful.

Important Business

All that has been said here about taste and excellence adds up to a sixth principle, not widely enough recognized but fundamental to good public relations and the raising of money: Every approach to every member of a college's total constituency should be pitched on the level of important business. If a man's support is important to an institution, if he is himself important, then the institution must attach genuine importance to the relationship with him. By and large, nothing is as good as a personal call by a responsible officer of the college. Failing that, all business by mail must be conducted with the utmost finesse. Here things that too often are given little weight have great importance: the quality of the stationery (or of the printed piece), the style of the address (and spelling the name right), the skill of the message, the person who signs it, the courtesy of the whole document.

Summary

Public relations consists of many and varied contacts between a college or university and its constituencies. The broad aim of a "PR" program is to gain prestige and to maintain goodwill.

Taste and selectiveness must be used in approaching the discriminating constituencies of higher education. They should be made to feel part of an institution, and be invited in to see it at work. The president inevitably is the chief representative of a college; he must take the lead as much in reaching its constituencies as in developing its educational program. His public relations officer must be in the inner circles of the administration, at least unofficially.

Seeking financial support from its various publics, a college must make a public accounting of its use of funds entrusted to it. Finally, every approach to every member of a college's total constituency should be pitched on the level of important business. A college that asks its friends to consider its opportunities and needs must itself be considerate.

REFERENCES

Chapter I

1. Clarence A. Schoenfeld, *The University and Its Publics* (New York: Harper & Brothers, 1954), p. 3.
2. Woodrow Wilson, *College and State: Educational, Literary and Political Papers, 1875–1913,* ed. by Ray Stannard Baker and William E. Dodd (New York and London: Harper & Brothers, 1925), Vol. I, p. 472.
3. E. B. Fred, "Productive Scholarship in Southern Colleges and Universities," Proceedings, *Southern University Conference, 1950* (Birmingham, Alabama: 1950), p. 76.
4. John D. Millett, "The Plight of the Private Liberal Arts College," an address to the Eighth Annual Institute of Higher Education, Scarritt College, Nashville, Tenn., July 24–26, 1951.
5. A. Lawrence Lowell, *What a University President Has Learned* (New York: The Macmillan Company, 1938), p. 12.
6. Schoenfeld, *op. cit.,* p. 173.
7. *A Study of Income and Expenditures in Sixty Colleges—Year 1953–1954* (New York: Columbia University Press, 1955), p. 3.
8. American Council on Education, *College and University Business Administration* (Washington, D.C., 1952), Vol. I, p. 34.
9. Institutions interested in improving their printing might read with profit Earl Schenck Miers' *Composing Sticks & Mortar Boards* (Camden, New Jersey: The Haddon Craftsmen, 1941). Mr. Miers observes, ". . . the catalogs, the bulletins and the announcements, the periodicals and the books which are coming from our universities and colleges too often are the reflection of hacks instead of artists. There is need for many awakenings." (p. 5.)

II
Building A Case
and a Constituency

Come, give us a taste of your quality.

—HAMLET

Good public relations helps to create the favorable setting in which to build a total constituency able to support a college adequately. Yet "PR" has definable limits. It is a distinct facility, but not a direct means of gaining such support. Only organized hard work will win it.

Establishing a Case

The institution's *case* is the nub of the matter. Securing adequate financing for the nation's colleges and universities has been so difficult as to seem to indicate a flaw in our society. Equally, however, this difficulty results from the fact that most of our colleges appear to do better at stretching out the needy hand than at putting forward the best foot.

This fact is stated succinctly by a man who has had more than thirty years of experience in educational fund-raising:

Few institutions competently present their cases. They may say they need endowment or buildings or both, but they fail to show (a) the over-all financial picture, and (b) exactly what would be accomplished if they received the needed funds. It is the exceptional case that is thoroughly and impressively documented.[1]

As a result of this fact, the history of many of our colleges and universities is dotted with instances of "the house out of order," bad feeling or lack of understanding among constituents, and resultant lack of support.

It is different when the sentiments between a college and its publics are grounded in trust and goodwill. The University of Chicago, reborn in 1892 with William Rainey Harper as its leader, began with the assurance of John D. Rockefeller's interest, but quickly won support from many and unexpected sources. In large part the reason was Harper's insistence on the basic principle of "service not merely to the students within its walls, but also to the public, to mankind." [2] Such were the enlightened acts of liberality by citizens toward the university that the trustees were "well-nigh bewildered by these exhibitions of public favor." [3]

Mr. Rockefeller comprehended the need for such good public relations leading to such support when he said, at the time in 1910 of making his "final gift" to the university, in the amount of $10 million:

It is far better that the University be supported by the gifts of many than by those of a single donor. . . . I am acting on an early and permanent conviction that this great institution, being the property of the people, should be controlled, conducted, and supported by the people, in whose generous efforts for its upbuilding I have been permitted simply to co-operate. . . . [4]

Perhaps even more significant, in its bearing on good public relations, is the story of the constituency of The Johns Hopkins University. When in 1896, twenty years after it opened its doors, the university suffered a complete loss of income on the major part of the endowment with which it had been founded by Johns Hopkins, it was tided over its day of peril by leading Baltimore businessmen and, for two years, even by annual grants of $50,000 from the Maryland legislature. Like President Harper at Chicago, Daniel Coit Gilman had won solid public confidence for the university over which he presided by dedicating it to purposes and services of large vision and scope. By 1902 the gifts of the people of Baltimore to the university, in money and land, had exceeded the value of the original bequest from Johns Hopkins.[5]

These instances, and a long list of others similar, illustrate an inflexible law, written and enforced by the experience of many centuries: Quality performance alone will attract adequate support to a college. A constituency from which support of this magnitude can be won will be built on one thing alone: A firm belief in the importance and quality of the service that the institution is giving to society. The institution's *case* is simply its record of service and accomplishment; or, in addition, its potential capacities in new fields of service that require to be explored.

Woodrow Wilson, when in December 1902 he announced to a New York dinner of Princeton alumni that he needed $2.5 million for the further development of the university, was able to state his case briefly: "Princeton has ever since her birthday stood for the service of the nation." [6] Wilson got his money.

More recently, between January 1948 and July 1951, Massachusetts Institute of Technology received $25 million as a means of increasing the quality and scope of its established service. Of major significance is the fact that 26 per cent of these new resources were given to M.I.T. by business and industrial corporations as an investment in its service to society —one of the greatest examples we have yet had of support by business of an institution of higher education.

It may be objected that these are merely instances of money attracting money. It is rather a case of success, in the highest sense, breeding success. Seldom does it fail that a college or university which succeeds in doing its essential work well succeeds also in finding a solid constituency and support. All of the institutions mentioned—including initially underwritten Chicago and Johns Hopkins and adding Cornell and Stanford —had to demonstrate excellence before they won broad support. Deeds and the case won dollars and the constituency.

Examples abound of colleges and universities that have had life-and-death struggles to survive and then have come up with spirit and *élan* sufficient to attract ardent supporters. Two examples will suffice.

Amherst College

No philanthropist, but individuals like Noah Webster, stood back of Amherst College in its beginnings (1821). The founders had to resort to "the community in general," and subscriptions ranged from about $3,000 down to six cents. Six years after the college was established it was $30,000 in debt. But when Edward Hitchcock became president in 1845 he worked out a scheme by which he and his faculty colleagues could carry forward the work of the college and receive what they might from tuitions. Also, the field agent whose solicitations had irritated the public was retired.

The results were almost magical. On the day Hitchcock was inaugurated, one benefactor gave $20,000 to endow a professorship. His gifts and those of one other philanthropic neighbor during the first year of the experiment seemed to Hitchcock to say: we will help those who are trying to help themselves. In two years Amherst received $108,000 in gifts from individuals impressed by the service which the impecunious college was giving. At the end of three years its finances were so greatly improved that the trustees paid with interest the arrears due the faculty on their salaries.

The high quality of Amherst's set of values attracted the two philanthropists. The college survived and became strong because, out of its early poverty, it produced excellence.

President Hitchcock later wrote one of the gospels of financing higher education: "Those only who have had the experience know how much more of money than is anticipated is required to start and carry onward and upward a literary institution of high character." [7]

Oberlin College

Oberlin offers, if possible, even better proof of how a good case wins a strong constituency. The town and gown of Oberlin were created together, in 1833, by a group of Christians who went out from New England to establish in the old Western Reserve a colony and an institution of Christian education. Great faith powered the movement, almost without the blessing of finance. At its opening the college had assets of less than $4,000 in subscriptions plus 500 acres of contributed land on which to build. Like so many other colleges founded during the expansion of the West it was a frail craft, and it came many times near to foundering before it reached safe harbor and a firm financial anchorage.

At the outset a scholarship scheme almost cost Oberlin its life. Even worse, large scale help proffered by a New York merchant was nullified by "acts of God." Agents combed the country for help, and yet by 1838 Oberlin was in debt, also by $30,000. This sum, considerable for an infant college at that time, was raised by two agents who were dispatched to the British Isles. Six years later the college was again deep in debt. Oberlin's fortunes continued to fluctuate precariously until a half century had passed, and then were stabilized by growing support from its graduates—none of them rich—and from friends who believed in its mission and were impressed by the quality of its service.

That service was indeed impressive. Oberlin students aided in the westward thrust of learning by helping to establish numerous other schools and colleges—Carleton, Drury, Grinnell, Hillsdale, Olivet, and Ripon among them.[8]

A Good Case Assures a Constituency

The case for an institution rests on its quality; on the whole measure of service which it renders to society; on the appropriateness of its educational program, both to itself and to the segment of society which it serves. When all is said and done, its case will rest on the degree to which its program prepares its graduates for choice service in the world.

All evidence makes it clear that an institution which performs well the rightful function of a college or university firmly establishes its case, and as surely enlists a total constituency that will support it. The constituency will be made up mainly of people whom it serves or has served: the alumni, business and industrial corporations, parents of present and former students, the professions, church denominations, civic groups, government at different levels, and even individuals —including trustees—who never have attended the institution but know the value of its service.

Gordon McKay, inventor and industrialist, never studied at Harvard (or at any other college), but by will he left it approximately $16.5 million in endowment. A few years ago Princeton was bequeathed about $1 million of the estate of Abram K. Wright, a Pennsylvania coal operator who had never been able to attend the university but admired it because of what it had contributed to the lives of two of his uncles and three cousins.

Results

The wise college, knowing that it constantly needs new funds for its growth and development, will devote care to making its case good and keeping it steadily clear in the view of all its constituencies. None but a well informed constituency can be appealed to successfully for support, and *only for a good case*.

Such a case can surely be built up by an institution of higher education that holds to its central purpose, the spread of learning and the discovery of new knowledge. When a college or university devotes its energies and resources to work that is appropriate to it—avoiding ruts of educational inertia, by-passing the quicksands of fads, skirting traditions that cloy, and searching with an alert eye for the better way ahead—it surely makes a case that will invite and indeed command confidence, a constituency, and cash.

If the institution is conducting its affairs well the good results will be evident:

Notable accomplishments of the faculty, and recognition among colleagues in their own and in other institutions.

High scholastic achievements among the students, both as undergraduates and in graduate and professional schools.

The successful lives of its alumni, chiefly as good citizens in leading the way toward the better quality of life which a democratic society always aspires to achieve.

The willingness of the highest type of people to serve actively as trustees.

The approval of the alumni, trustees, and other friends closest to it, as shown by their liberality in giving it funds which an alert institution will always need.

Samuel E. Morison wrote perceptively, in his *Three Centuries of Harvard:* "It was not inevitable that Harvard should become a great university; the wisdom and devotion of countless people have furthered the process. . . ." [9]

In the United States in 1957 there were about 1,870 colleges, universities, professional schools, and two-year or community colleges. Some careful observers fear that not all of the privately financed institutions may survive the effects of today's inflation and rising costs. But it is difficult to believe that in a country with a current personal income totaling around $345 billion annually, money cannot be found to support all of the institutions of higher education which are doing their chosen work well.

Now and then false sentiment leads benefactors to make unwise gifts. Today, every circumstance attending philanthropy underscores the need for a good case back of any college or university that seeks large funds. Corporation giving, zealously prayed for and slowly increasing in amount, is likely to add a note of even more hard-headed realism to philanthropy, and to put still greater emphasis on the need for a good case.

REFERENCES

Chapter II

1. David M. Church, Executive Director, The American Association of Fund-Raising Counsel.
2. Thomas Wakefield Goodspeed, *The Story of the University of Chicago, 1890–1925* (Chicago: The University of Chicago Press, 1925), p. 55.
3. *Ibid.,* p. 131.
4. *Ibid.,* p. 179.
5. John C. French, *A History of the University Founded by Johns Hopkins* (Baltimore: The Johns Hopkins Press, 1946), pp. 99, 101.
6. Woodrow Wilson, *College and State: Educational, Literary and Political Papers, 1875–1913,* ed. by Ray Stannard Baker and William E. Dodd (New York and London: Harper & Brothers, 1925), Vol. I, p. 472.
7. Edward Hitchcock, *Reminiscences of Amherst College* (Northampton: Bridgman & Childs, 1863), pp. 118, 122, 125, 126, 133, 117.
8. James H. Fairchild, *Oberlin: the Colony and the College* (Oberlin, E. J. Goodrich, 1883), pp. 9–10, 24, 149, 150, 152, 205, 208, 209, 210, 212, 215.
9. Samuel E. Morison, *Three Centuries of Harvard* (Cambridge: Harvard University Press, 1937), p. 89.

III Leadership and Teamwork

Doänt thou marry for munny,
but goä wheer munny is!

—TENNYSON, *Northern Farmer, New Style*

Once it has solidly built up its case and its constituency, a college or university is in a good way to attract funds. But the prime fact about raising money is that it is necessary to ask for it. In our country, devoted like no other in the world to the practice of private philanthropy, it has been necessary at all times and all levels to press the case.

Someone has said rightly that in fund-raising, the best means of communication is shoe leather.

Cases in Point

Raising money for social institutions has long appealed to leading citizens as both an opportunity and a responsibility. Washington gave $50,000 to what is now Washington and Lee University. Franklin and Jefferson gave time, thought, and treasure to the universities which they helped to found. And in their own special ways the great nineteenth-century philanthropists were leaders in helping colleges and universities of their choice.

Yet beyond comparison the best leadership in fund-raising for these institutions has come, naturally, from the ranks of people who have lived and worked closest to them. Henry Dunster, President of Harvard from 1642 to 1654, and John Witherspoon, President of Princeton from 1768 to 1794, established the principle that financial support for a college must be found among many people. In equal parts they were builders, salvage experts, and scholars possessed of a strong religious drive. Genuinely inspired leadership of the kind they furnished was generated also among the sponsors of Bowdoin, Marietta, Middlebury, Mount Holyoke, Williams, and other colleges founded during a later period but in the same penury.

UNIVERSITY OF ROCHESTER

In the development of the University of Rochester common lessons are pointed up. At its start in 1850, advocates of the university went after subscriptions and got more than $140,-000 from over 800 individuals. Three business leaders who enjoyed prestige and influence in Rochester were in the van of this effort. Hiram Sibley in 1871 gave the first large sum, $75,000 for the improvement of the library.

George Eastman's interest, stirred by the growing quality of the university located in his home city, evidently began in 1903 with a gift to provide for erecting the biology-physics laboratory building. Ultimately his interest in the university took the expression of direct gifts to it in the amount of something like $25 million. Moreover, his leadership resulted in the winning of other large sums from friendly sources, including approximately $7 million in grants from the General Education Board.[1]

UNIVERSITY OF CHICAGO

An even more impressive demonstration of the value of vigorous leadership and teamwork was given at Chicago, and it gains in significance from the fact that it was staged on ground where there had been a previous failure. Repeatedly hit by catastrophes, the first University of Chicago had lived from 1856 to 1886. The reborn university, child of John D. Rockefeller and the Baptist Education Board, was attended into the world by two wonder men of academic fund-raising, Frederick T. Gates and Thomas W. Goodspeed. (Gates was later to take his considerable talents into the Rockefeller Foundation and the General Education Board.)

Mr. Rockefeller's original gift, the first in a long series that extended to 1910 and totaled approximately $35 million, was in the amount of $600,000. Made in 1890, it was contingent on the raising of $400,000 more from other sources in one year's time. This was spur enough to Gates and Goodspeed. From Baptist people they got contributions of $233,000 in Chicago and $116,000 outside the city. Businessmen of Chicago, including Field and later Ryerson, gave the two leaders $200,000 on a $100,000 quota. During the year ending June 1890 they had secured subscriptions totaling $549,000.

Gates and Goodspeed were just getting their stride. Helped along meanwhile by two additional gifts of $1 million each from Mr. Rockefeller, they led a campaign among Chicago citizens which in ninety days added $1 million in subscriptions for buildings. Before the new University of Chicago opened its doors in the autumn of 1892, it had a large and improved site, cash in the amount of $4 million, and provision for ten buildings.[2] Considering time and circumstances, there has been no other single equal demonstration of the value of leadership and teamwork in fund-raising for higher education.*

Naturally, the strength of the case helped, too

Portrait of a Leader

William Lawrence, Episcopal Bishop of Massachusetts from 1893 to 1926, was first a citizen and then a churchman. His most appropriate title would have been Minister Extraordinary and Envoy Plenipotentiary, for that is what in the full-

---

* The fact that, despite all this brilliant achievement, the University of Chicago from the day it opened had a fifteen-year struggle with deficits, merely underscores—as do the Cornell, Johns Hopkins, and Stanford stories—the tremendous cost of launching an institution of higher education, especially a first class university.

est sense he was. Bishop Lawrence was a power, able to approach any man on equal terms or to enlist virtually anybody in an enterprise to which he was supplying leadership. More than that, he distilled principles out of his extensive money-raising experience, principles as valid today as when he first put them on paper.

Although he pleaded "inexperience in raising money," Bishop Lawrence was impressed to take the lead in a movement of 1904–1905 to raise $2.5 million additional endowment for Harvard College faculty salaries. The Bishop learned remarkably fast, Harvard received its new funds, and Lawrence had from that time what he later called "an invigorating avocation." [3]

In 1914 Bishop Lawrence led the Wellesley "team" in a remarkable recovery from the effects of a fire which in March destroyed the college's main building. As chairman of the board of trustees, Lawrence was persuaded to take the lead in raising money for a building to replace Stone Hall. He went first to New York, to see John D. Rockefeller, Jr. and Wallace Buttrick. At Mr. Rockefeller's suggestion Lawrence set a goal of $2 million, whereupon the Rockefeller Foundation made a pledge of $750,000 contingent upon Wellesley's raising the remainder from its own sources.

On January 1, 1915, the college announced that the $2 million goal had been reached, plus $430,000 which had been conditionally subscribed to Wellesley before the time of the fire.

Bishop Lawrence next devoted his talents to the Episcopal Church Pension Fund, the first such fund ever raised in the United States. With the help of J. P. Morgan and other individuals, and of the Carnegie Corporation of New York, Lawrence and his colleagues accumulated $8.75 million for the Fund by September 1917. Every step they took was over new territory.

In 1922 the Bishop led a movement, with a slogan of Spiritual Leadership, which raised $1 million for the Episcopal Theological School.

Then followed what was eminently his most successful leadership of a team effort—to procure $10 million in new funds for the Harvard Graduate School of Business Administration. Bishop Lawrence now did the logical but imaginative thing of making an office in Wall Street his temporary headquarters. He labored, it is true, in the friendly shadow of Trinity Church, but he was also at ease with financial potentates. Assured by the astute Ivy Ledbetter Lee that *facts* would state the case best, Bishop Lawrence was brief in his calls. In one notably short interview with George F. Baker, he insured the success of this first "campaign" ever sanctioned by the Corporation of Harvard University. Bishop Lawrence stated his case, suggested that Mr. Baker think about the possibility of giving the first million toward the fund, and departed. Mr. Baker thought, not for long, and contributed $5 million.[4]

Lawrence's Principles

What principles of money-raising did Bishop Lawrence follow, or discover?

First of all, he led people to do "voluntarily" what he wanted them to do for causes in which he was interested. He concluded that "men are prone to give in behalf of their own discoveries."

And *facts* are of fundamental importance. Reflecting on the raising of the Harvard College endowment of $2.5 million, Lawrence wrote:

To educate the friends of the University in the value of what I have always called "spiritual vitality" was one of our chief duties; and I am more and more clear that when this idea is rightly expressed, the response is more intelligent and generous than for buildings.[5]

Bishop Lawrence's procedure was to set the facts before a prospect, take no pledge from him, and let the person decide for himself what he could and should do. While at work on the Episcopal Church Pension Fund he would call on a selected prospect, leave a copy of the pamphlet, "The Plan," along with a list of the heaviest subscribers to date, and let the person think on the matter.

Leadership and teamwork, he knew as well as any man, are the unfailing keys to success in fund-raising. He believed that the leaders of a campaign must first ask themselves just how much the institution needs, and also how much the constituency is likely to give to it. "Before you can get support," he wrote, "you must be sure that you have a good cause, one that stands on its own feet." And he summed up his whole experience of the garnering of money when he emphasized:

The great purpose, however, which is sometimes lost in the whirring of wheels, is to touch sympathetically multitudes of people; and the best organization is that which, having power and system at its heart, keeps its outmost workers as sensitive as the nerves beneath the finger-tips.[6]

That is excellent fund-raising doctrine, well tested by time, ably stated by Bishop Lawrence and skillfully applied by leaders before and after him who have borne financial cares for colleges and universities and all other types of social institutions. Lawrence achieved such spectacular successes partly, it is manifest, because of his potent connections. But, in essence, the principles that guided him also guided Dunster, Witherspoon, Shipherd and Stewart (Oberlin), Gates and Goodspeed, and a long line of other men and women who have dedicated themselves to the problem of procuring adequate financing for higher education.

Fund-Raising Presidents

Fund-raising is probably distasteful to most college presidents. Yet many have regarded it as a necessary game to be played, and some have played it extremely well. Dr. Donald J. Cowling, at Carleton, set his educational sights clear and high and demonstrated unusual capacity for getting funds to support his program.[7] Dr. Frank Aydelotte is generally credited with having accomplished as much for Swarthmore. His prestige and that of the college insured an open door and a thoughtful hearing, and led to good results. Nicholas Murray Butler through his personal efforts and connections raised perhaps as much as $100 million for Columbia University during his long presidency.

One president who evidently did get some pleasure from his fund-raising labors was able to leaven them with humor, and his account of them is pointed with useful lessons. Henry Noble MacCracken, during his thirty-one-year presidency of Vassar—a time, he says, that "witnessed great gifts to education"—helped to increase the college's assets in plant and endowment from $5 million to $25 million. Yet he felt that in a relative way Vassar lost ground, in large part because he never made fund-raising a primary concern.

At his inauguration Dr. MacCracken chose his old Harvard instructor, George Lyman Kittredge, to make the appropriate personal address. Kittredge knew how to deal with facts. He stated that although Vassar had a scholar for its new president, the real nature of the job was to raise money. And Kittredge compared a college president to the parson in the Prologue to the Canterbury Tales: ". . . though his parish, like that of Chaucer's parson, is 'wide, with houses far asunder,' he is expected to visit them all, 'upon his feet, and in his hand a staff.' "

Of his new vocation Dr. MacCracken was to write: "It is not a business for the sensitive, or the shy, or the impatient. It is, I think, only endurable when it is taken as a sport (stalking deer is the nearest parallel) or as an art." [8]

During his first month in office Dr. MacCracken was prompted by the alumnae to seek $1 million in fresh funds, and together they created a campaign organization, without professional counsel. Happily, seeds planted by his predecessor came to fruition during the early years of MacCracken's administration in a number of large gifts from individual alumnae. Again, the total giving of the alumnae, who organized Vassar's annual fund in 1915, was stimulated by contingent gifts from foundations, among them a grant of $200,-000 from the General Education Board. While conferring with officers of the board, MacCracken received this sovereign advice from one of its members, Wickliff Rose: "When you are hunting for money, use a rifle, not a shotgun. You'll be more likely to bring down your game."

With respect to individuals, MacCracken had good aim indeed. From some came what he must have regarded as uncovenanted blessings, but all were undoubtedly the result of skilled cultivation. Charles M. Pratt of the Standard Oil Company sent to MacCracken, by messenger and without previous announcement, a package containing railroad bonds worth $100,000. On another occasion the grandmother of a Vassar student sent the president an engraved cigarette case, ostensibly a gift for his birthday, in which was a check made out to the college for $10,000. At a luncheon she had asked him how much he wanted her to contribute to the Chicago alumnae quota of Vassar's Seventy-Fifth Anniversary Fund. He had replied, "Whatever you will."

Equally noteworthy is the fact that from the outset MacCracken was able to count upon the interest and participation of the alumnae in all of his labors on behalf of Vassar. With respect to the Fiftieth Anniversary Fund he wrote, "It seemed as if the alumnae were just waiting to be asked." The heavy work was carried on by the organization of class secretaries. In 1922 the alumnae subscribed $2 million to insure collecting John D. Rockefeller's contingent half million. And finally, in 1940, the Seventy-Fifth Anniversary Fund of $2 million was completed on the last day.

MacCracken's Advice

What rules does President MacCracken consider to apply to this "deer stalking" occupation? They are few but essential, and they have a familiar ring of experience.

1. "Any large gift ought to be allowed to ripen on the tree." Approximately ten years was the average time for fruition. Knowledge of the college, sharing in its life from time to time, and personal contact with students and faculty motivated contributions. But the idea of the gift is the donor's own, and the time and the form in which he makes it are for him to decide. President MacCracken cannot recall that he actually asked for more than one large gift. Thus big gifts spring, ultimately, from well informed contacts, both casual and planned. Mac-Cracken concludes that you don't get large gifts, "they grow out of experience."

2. Gifts in smaller amounts greatly outweigh and outnumber large benefactions. MacCracken estimated that $100,000 gifts to Vassar do not total $10 million, while smaller gifts come to at least $15 million. And he adds, "Not only are the smaller gifts, most of them at a hundred or two hundred dollars, more significant in the mass; they mean more to the college in other ways." He instances a scholarship fund built up by a missionary in India in his wife's memory, through small amounts given over many years of service.

3. Vassar's mass drives were useful in training Vassar leaders for other social leadership.

4. Not all gifts can be accepted by an independent college. Gifts that might influence its management by the president, trustees, and faculty are unacceptable.

5. The annual fund is a means of nurturing and sustaining

interest among graduates, especially those living in places at some distance from the college. (Vassar's mass drives cost only 3 per cent in overhead operation. The average cost for the most successful annual funds is 10 to 12 per cent.)

6. You can't please everybody.

Quay's Advice

One other individual representative who has recently set down helpful notes on his craft is James King Quay, former Vice-President of the Princeton Theological Seminary. Mr. Quay underscores the fact that gifts are made rather in terms of the donor's interest in the institution than in what the institution desires to get from him.[9] He advises fund-raisers never to forget a basic law influencing human behavior: "The gardener does not lay down the law to the rosebush; the rosebush lays down the law to the gardener."

Mr. Quay makes other useful suggestions, bearing chiefly upon attitude and finesse. He counsels strongly against a begging approach to a prospective contributor, and emphasizes that it requires time and a number of calls or interviews to cultivate his interest and to create the basis for his wanting to give. Because any person with a high sense of stewardship is unlikely to have large uncommitted funds ready to dispose of, Mr. Quay has found that the wise fund-raiser will not expect an immediate "yes," but will be prepared tactfully to turn a "no" into the foundation for a gift later. If pressure is not at once applied, and if the individual is left free to form his own judgment, the initial interview is more likely to lead to a "yes" in time.

Appropriately, Mr. Quay lays stress on having respect for the man you approach—first of all, on learning in advance "his enthusiasms, his prejudices, his giving ability, his giving habits, the particular features in your cause which he may not like, as well as those that are likely to appeal to him, the friends he has or the people he respects who already support your work."

In the second place, this kind of approach means crediting your prospect with being a man of generous impulses. Mr. Quay has found it best, in the first interview, merely to present the need of his cause and the opportunity to give to it. Best practice, in Mr. Quay's experience, is to follow the first interview with printed material and other supporting measures such as invitations to campus events and the letter of thanks for the interview, as well as the friendly word spoken to the prospect by a friend of his who is already one of your contributors.

Above all, Mr. Quay underscores the necessity of leading with your best card. Arranging for a personal interview under the most favorable auspices is a "must," even though getting it may require a year. Specifically, Mr. Quay believes, "somehow a friend of the prospect must be found to pave the way for you with a personal word, a telephone call, or a letter."

Mr. Quay ventures several other canons:

1. Be sure you try to "sell" the right thing.
2. Be tactfully persistent.
3. Make your appeal concrete.
4. Keep the prospect list growing.
5. Don't take money for nothing. Use every opportunity to let a man or woman enjoy the satisfaction of large-hearted giving. It is wise to call on him or communicate with him occasionally when you are not in a seeking mood. Here Mr. Quay touches a sensitive point familiar to any experienced fund-raiser: the courtesy of reminding a donor of what his gift is accomplishing in your institution is mandatory.
6. Don't overlook foundations and corporations. (These are covered in detail in Chapters X and XI of this book.)

Men like MacCracken and Quay have realized fully that fund-raising for a college or university is a basic, never-ending function; and to this extent they and other "agents" have helped to lay the basis for the continuous campaign. But their work has been limited by the amount which they as individuals could do, and by the additional amount which they could get from the few volunteers who helped to undergird their work. This work needed to be broadened and intensified.

Summary

One comprehensive and cardinal principle lies at the root of the most notable fund-raising achievements: no appeal for support can be made effectively without a good case, first rate leadership, and co-workers thoroughly committed to the cause and willing to go to the right sources and ask for money.

The prime fact about raising money is that one has to ask for it.

Raising money for social institutions appeals to leading citizens as an opportunity and a responsibility. It is gratifying to be identified with important work.

Solicitation of funds for a college or university is not begging. It is helping to build up an important institution.

The best leadership in raising funds for a college comes naturally from among people who live and work closest to it.

Financial support for a college or university must be found among many people. And many people must help to find it.

Facts will command their interest.

"Any large gift ought to be allowed to ripen on the tree." It takes time to mature, and will be made in terms of the donor's interest in the institution.

The value of large numbers of small gifts is likely to surpass the value of a small number of large gifts to a college.

Compile careful information about a large-gift prospect before you go near him. Credit him with being a person of generous impulses. Arrange to see him under the best possible auspices.

Be sure you try to sell the right thing, and make your appeal concrete.

Don't take money for nothing. And practice the courtesy of reminding a donor of what his gift is accomplishing for your institution.

REFERENCES

Chapter III

1. Jesse Leonard Rosenberger, *Rochester, The Making of a University* (Rochester: The University of Rochester, 1927), pp. 47, 278, *passim*.
2. Thomas Wakefield Goodspeed, *The Story of the University of Chicago, 1890–1925* (Chicago: The University of Chicago Press, 1925), pp. 2, 23, *passim*.
3. William Lawrence, "An Invigorating Avocation," *The Atlantic Monthly*, September 1923, pp. 317–323.
4. William Lawrence, *Memories of a Happy Life* (Boston and New York: Houghton Mifflin Co., 1926), p. 214, *passim*.
5. *Ibid.*, p. 217.
6. William Lawrence, "An Invigorating Avocation," *op. cit.*, p. 322.
7. Although his carefully devised program of development for Carleton College is now more than a quarter-century old, Dr. Cowling's method of the study of educational needs remains a model. See his "How Much Money Does a College Need?" *School and Society*, July 5, 1930, pp. 6–10.
8. This brief record of President MacCracken's fund-raising experiences is based on his *The Hickory Limb* (New York: Charles Scribner's Sons, 1950), Chapter 13.
9. James King Quay, "The Romance and the Technic of Raising Money," *College and University Business*, October 1952, pp. 19–21.

IV   The Corps of Volunteers

> Then seek your job with thankfulness and
> work till further orders,
> If it's only netting strawberries or killing
> slugs on borders;
> And when your back stops aching and your
> hands begin to harden,
> You will find yourself a partner in the Glory
> of the Garden.
>
> —KIPLING, *The Glory of the Garden*

How to identify, enlist, train, make effective, and hold voluntary co-workers is a puzzle to many college and university
heads. Actually, there are tested and proved guidelines for
moving from the "power and system" to the "outmost workers."

First of all, as Bishop Lawrence demonstrated, it is necessary to have a clear purpose for a fund-raising appeal. If it is
sound, volunteers will join the team. The purpose of any well
conceived campaign for money is *friend-raising* as well as
fund-raising. It is to buttress confidence in the work of the institution, with the certainty that understanding precedes giving.

Solicitation of funds for a college or university is not begging; it is helping to build up an important social institution.
John Masefield has said, "There are few things more splendid
than a University . . . more enduring . . . more beautiful." [1]

Among most alumni there is an added attitude or sentiment, well expressed by Helen H. Couch, of Vassar College:

And this, in the final analysis, is what you are after. It is the

affection that your alumnae have for your college and their loyalty
to and faith in what your college stands for—these are the things,
which are primarily emotional, that make your fund program successful. Though your alumnae may have made a thoughtful evalua-
tion of why education and why the education your particular college gives is important, continuing healthy giving is, primarily,
more a matter of the heart than it is of the mind.[2]

Being engaged in important work like the strengthening of
a college or university appeals to most men and women,
whether alumni or not. Participation in such work identifies a
person with the institution, and this identification pushes him
on to productive efforts in its behalf.

Recruitment

Recruitment is the business of the ranking officers of the
development program or the alumni fund, as the case may be,
with the assistance of the paid staff. In some instances, as at
Occidental College and Rensselaer Polytechnic Institute, the
chairman of the development program is not an alumnus.

In such a program it is highly advantageous to have trustee
participation. This gives trustees a continuing assignment in
fund-raising, and keeps them in touch with its problems. Their
influence is useful in bringing into the program new members
of high quality. And the enterprise takes on added prestige
because of the trustees' part in it. Lehigh and Occidental,
among many other educational institutions, believe in this
tenet of fund-raising and practice it.

Lehigh's periodic capital gifts campaigns (two in the last
ten years), her annual alumni fund, and her business and industry program are all built on personal solicitation by volunteer workers. In a normal year the university has approximately 500 volunteer solicitors working on its behalf. In a special year involving a capital-gifts campaign this figure goes
well over 2,000.

Most of these workers are enlisted in the manner commonly employed in capital-gifts campaigns. Lehigh begins with a trustee or some other prominent Lehigh alumnus as chairman of a group. He enlists five topflight assistants or captains, and they in turn enlist numerous teams of five workers each. Volunteers enlist volunteers.

Lehigh, like other colleges and universities, tries to steer the recruitment in the right direction by providing the lists of people from among whom the volunteers can pick their co-workers, and by insuring that these lists contain the university's best prospects as well as its best workers. Lehigh's periodic capital-gifts campaigns give it an opportunity to uncover new individuals who prove to be excellent workers and givers.

The Ohio State University Development Fund, old among state university funds, had 711 volunteer workers in Columbus alone, its home city, during its 1956 campaign. Ohio State's volunteers are reported to fall into three categories:

1. Those who have worked every year since the fund was started in 1939. These people are described as "loyalists who actually would be offended if they were not asked to work each year."

2. Those who are enthusiastic about the fund and will work well and effectively for about five or six years. Then they like to be relieved.

3. Those who do it one year only, find it is a job they do not enjoy, and do not want to do it another year.

Yale University estimates that it has between 5,000 and 7,000 alumni voluntarily engaged in one enterprise or another that has to do with the financing of the university: the Alumni (annual) Fund, the Alumni Board (clubs and associations), the Class Secretaries, and the Yale Development Committee (special gifts). Eighty-three men were invited to join the Yale Development Committee; eighty accepted, and the other three had valid excuses.

Training

Most college development programs are long range. So there is not the intensive, high-pressure sales direction which is to be found in charity drives or in commercial enterprises. The main job is to provide the volunteer worker with facts, sales aids, and plans for special projects in areas where he can use them, and to keep him in close contact with the college, and recognize his good work.

Nonetheless, "sales direction" or training is important, even essential, for voluntary workers in annual funds.

Various colleges and universities give this training in various ways. Evidently it has best effect when it can be given on the campus. Ohio State and Yale, to name only two universities, put on carefully planned programs of indoctrination on their campuses, Yale during the autumn and Ohio State in winter.

At Columbus, the Development Fund Workshop is attended by the chairmen who will lead the personal solicitation in various parts of the country. Almost 100 per cent of the chairmen attend. First scheduled is a morning session at which complete details are given about the mechanics of conducting a campaign of personal solicitation for gifts. At luncheon, on the campus, the president or one of the vice presidents of the university greets the volunteers on its behalf. During the afternoon the visiting group are taken to see two or three projects or places on the campus which have been aided by development fund monies. This part of the workshop appears to be the most valuable. Demonstrating to the volunteers some of the research projects that have been financed by the development fund is not only interesting but appears to create considerable enthusiasm.

Following dinner, also on the campus, the local fund chairmen are taken to a basketball game or some other athletic event. It rounds out a day's program well balanced between hard work and pleasure. Local chairmen are reported to return home inspired. The growing effectiveness of The Ohio State University Development Fund—in 1956 it received $800,144 in annual gifts from 25,254 donors, including 23,-783 alumni—is proof of the training.

Vassar College adds a note of experience. The volunteers should be called together as soon as practicable, preferably on home territory. The "general objective must be to inspire confidence . . . and to create in them enthusiasm and pride for what they are doing." [3]

Nature of the Fund Program

In most cases the objectives toward which the volunteers are invited to work will have to be interpreted by professionals —the president, the development officer, the alumni secretary, or some other person situated in the institution. It is necessary to have distinct objectives. They have to be explained in specific, not general, terms; in terms that make clear the kind of educational job the college is trying to do and the kind of income it must have in order to do a job of that quality. Merely speaking of a budget of one, two, five or more millions that must be raised from all sources is vague. It is likely to be also bewildering.

Again Vassar speaks with the voice of experience:

But if you spell this [budget] out in terms of how many tons of food are consumed each week, . . . in terms of the faculty salary level and how the college hopes this may be raised—if, in other words, you are specific, the financial needs will be far more obvious. [4]

The next step is to measure, against its total budget, the possible sources of income for the college, and in turn to measure the gap that must be closed. Usually it is necessary to emphasize the obvious: that "the first possibility of support lies immediately with the alumni." And "then define the structure of your fund program. Do it so that the structure becomes realistic and so that the goals represent something that can be achieved step by step." [5]

Occidental College, in its long-range development program, also has specific short-term objectives to which, from time to time and according to their own special interests, the members of the President's Associates (approximately two hundred in number) direct their attention.

The Individual Load

How much actual soliciting each volunteer should be asked to do varies from college to college. But in order to hold workers from year to year it is important not to overload them. George J. Cooke, Jr., of the Princeton University Fund, says, "Ideally, each worker should have one card—his own." In practice, Princeton works on the basis of five calls to a worker.

Ohio State University gives each worker a relatively small number of calls to make, close to his or her home or office. They know from experience that seven calls is about the right number for each solicitor. Fund officers caution local chairmen not to give any worker more than ten calls to make unless some special consideration is involved.

Quotas are employed by some universities and colleges, rejected by others. Where the solicitation is geared more to geographical areas or to professional school affiliations than to undergraduate class membership, quotas are a useful mechanism. Vassar, for one, however, avoids arbitrary goals, for it finds that the individual classes produce much the best results if left to set their own sights. Equally, the college gives individual solicitors room of their own in which to operate: "Men and women who are asked to assume responsibility, who are given the reins in their own hands, rise to that responsibility." [6]

Making the Wheels Go Round

Numerous colleges and universities prepare manuals for the use of their fund-raising operations. Dartmouth, as an example, has annually for a number of years issued a printed guidebook, brief and pocket-sized, including do's and dont's for its solicitors. Ohio State issues multilithed manuals both for the local chairmen and for the team workers. Lehigh gives instructions to its solicitors both orally and in printed form.

Occidental College has gone one step further and has prepared, for the use of members of the President's Associates, a "sales manual." It is a leather-bound looseleaf folder containing the main sales points about the desirability of giving to an educational institution, to a liberal arts college, and specifically to Occidental. The pages are hand-lettered, the messages brief and illustrated with cartoons. Included are quotations from men of national prominence and influence, and summary material about Occidental.

Like numerous other institutions, Lehigh University begins all of its campaigns with area kick-off meetings, for reasons partly instructional and partly inspirational. After ten years' experience, Lehigh finds these annual meetings useful because new workers are constantly being recruited. Even the university's class agents, rated old hands at money-raising, are brought together once a year in New York City for a meeting at which the fundamentals of getting gifts are reviewed and stressed. And each year the class agents receive a special manual which tells them about their job and how to prepare class letters: what to say and what not to say.

The Ohio State University Development Fund also finds area kick-off meetings useful in the training of team workers. No way has yet been discovered of convening them all at the same time. Whenever possible the fund makes the meeting a complimentary dinner, as in Cleveland, where an alumnus who is a prominent industrialist pays the bill. Even with this bait, only about 75 per cent of the area solicitors can be counted upon to attend, since no date is ever convenient for 100 per cent. But Ohio State finds that the new workers usually attend these kick-off meetings, and the veterans know their lines.

As for report meetings, experience and opinions differ. There is common agreement that periodic reporting is indispensable, as a gauge both of progress made and of what remains to be done. Lehigh finds report meetings more effective than any other medium in spurring solicitors to see their prospects. Report cards can be mailed to area workers, but campaign headquarters may get no reply. Lehigh has learned that holding area report meetings once a week for three weeks really gets results.

While holding to deadlines, Lehigh also emphasizes campaign bulletins: weekly lists of the workers, the gifts they have reported, the prospects they have not seen. Competition is promoted among areas, classes, and individuals. Prizes are awarded for meritorious performance.

Rensselaer Polytechnic Institute also finds that an orderly reporting of the results they are helping to achieve is an excellent means of keeping volunteer workers active and enthusiastic. It also issues a well printed, condensed "Development Newsletter" periodically. R.P.I. has learned that "a good principle is to see that as many volunteers as possible share in a victory. Who can tell which word, which argument, or which favorable attitude was the straw that swung the gift to the college?" The institute's development office finds value also in luncheon meetings, dutch-treat affairs, held if possible on the campus and attended by members of the staff and by volunteers.

Ohio State avoids a multiplicity of meetings. In addition to the kick-off meeting, the only other gathering of area workers and their chairmen is a final report meeting. Many solicitors have said to fund headquarters: "Certainly, I would be glad to work for the development fund, but just don't ask me to come to a lot of meetings."

On the other hand Occidental College, working through the President's Associates for capital gifts with which to reach its long-range objectives, holds numerous luncheons and dinners on the campus as a means of presenting its case. The President's Associates hold four dinners a year on the campus and one formal dinner off campus. In October of 1957 the Associates arranged a special on-campus dinner at which President A. G. Coons presented the college's long-range development plan, with special reference to Occidental's seventy-fifth anniversary in 1962.

Established friends and potential friends of the college are invited to special luncheons by the President's Associates and by committees of the faculty, of the alumni, and of other groups interested in Occidental's growth. The "sales manual" including flip-charts, already referred to, is used by the director of development at these campus meetings. No direct appeal for funds is made at these affairs, but the Occidental story is explained, as well as the college's opportunity and needs to fulfill its appropriate role in state and nation.

Careful cultivation of individual prospects is geared into this program. Cultivation is carried on steadily, not by the president alone but by the development fund staff and by any individuals whose aid can be enlisted in appropriate ways.

Role of the Paid Staff

Rensselaer Polytechnic Institute believes the most important thing of all, in using volunteers effectively, is to get the proper perspective between the volunteer and the development office. The volunteer is not helping the development office to look good; it is the other way round. It is the job of the office to stay in the background, to do the clerical, statistical, and leg work, and to have resulting material available to the volunteer worker even before he knows he is going to need it. There is work that he alone can do, but proper staff preparation may make it 80 to 90 per cent easier for him.

Making such a plan work requires continuing personal contact between members of the development office staff and the volunteer workers. This contact may be maintained by letter or by telephone or, better, by brief personal calls once a month. With the volunteer chairman, of course, closer contact must be maintained.

Along with R.P.I., Lehigh, Occidental, Ohio State, and others know the value of personal calls on volunteers. All of these institutions underscore the fact that volunteers cannot be driven.

The Harvard Fund (annual fund of Harvard College) still has four of its original class agents, appointed in 1925, and would have more if death had not intervened. Class agents like to call at Wadsworth House, headquarters of the Harvard Fund Council, or to keep in touch by telephone. The fund council staff tries to follow the wishes of each agent, so long as they are consonant with the larger aims of the Fund.

Vassar puts the matter in a nutshell: "We urge on these volunteers the feeling that *they* are the executives. Somebody else will do the routine work and will cope with the details. They are the masters." [7]

Recognition
The considerateness emphasized in Chapter I is nowhere more important for a college than in its relations with voluntary workers. Harvard invites its corps to an annual dinner in the Fogg Museum of Art. The president and the dean are nearly always on hand, and the university puts on "an uncommonly pleasant program with excellent food." The executive secretary of the fund council comments: "I don't say that

this is what holds the Agents together, but since it is our one chance to assemble under a single roof, it must be a large factor."

Lehigh tries "to give any solicitor for Lehigh a little publicity somewhere along the line." It considers letters of thanks important, especially if signed by the chairman of the campaign or the president of the university. Year after year Lehigh goes back to the same group of men asking them to serve as heads or members of its numerous committees. Few are reluctant to continue serving. An officer of the university explains why:

I think perhaps they like the work. We have consistently made our goals, they have consistently felt part of a winning team. They are looked up to as leaders in their alumni community—they feel that they have done something for Lehigh and higher education. In certain of our areas there is something in the way of social prestige that creeps into the picture.[8]

Rensselaer Polytechnic Institute adds a refinement worth noting. It has a faculty committee on reports and appreciation that not only reports and expresses appreciation to donors for their gifts, but to volunteers also. Recently the student honorary society elected the development program's chairman to membership because of what the program had done for the students on the campus. For outstanding work two other leaders in the development program have been elected to the R.P.I. Board of Trustees.

It is a good thing to tell a volunteer that what he is doing is important to the college. It is even better to *act* to show that it is.

In special ways Vassar gives stellar booking to workers in its alumnae fund. During an annual campaign it finds that the psychology of giving them something "for free" is magical. At commencement, on the Sunday of reunion weekend, the college features a fund meeting by itself. In 1955 the meeting went on for two hours and drew 900 women to the biggest room on the Vassar campus. "A meeting like this can really become a dramatic performance," an officer of the alumnae fund has said, and Vassar makes it so.[9]

Growing Into Larger Roles

As at Rensselaer Polytechnic Institute, some volunteers at other colleges and universities come up through the ranks into positions of institutional leadership. An officer of the Ohio State University Development Fund reports: "By getting these alumni to work for the University we are binding them closer to it and developing in them an enthusiasm for the University which nothing else seems to do as effectively. . . . Personal solicitation is the 'basic training' for officership."

It can also be a springboard to leadership in the broader walks of life. On the basis of his presidency at Poughkeepsie, Henry Noble MacCracken wrote that "our drives were valuable to Vassar leaders in training them for other social leadership. Many of our workers have become well known in different phases of American life as a result of this training." [10]

Summary

Recruitment of volunteer workers requires strong leadership, best stemming from the trustees.

Once a team is started, volunteers enlist volunteers.

A clear plan and objectives must be placed before them, and their work facilitated by the paid staff of the development fund or alumni fund.

No individual solicitor should be asked to make more than five to seven calls.

Periodic reporting of work accomplished is necessary to maintaining confidence and enthusiasm among workers.

Recognition in word and in act must, with scrupulous care, be given to volunteer workers.

References

Chapter IV

1. In an address by Masefield at the University of Sheffield, England, June 1946.
2. Helen H. Couch, "How to Make the Most Effective Use of Volunteers," in *The "How to" of Educational Fund Raising* (Washington, D.C.: The American Alumni Council, January 1956), p. 51.
3. *Ibid.,* p. 46.
4. *Ibid.,* p. 47.
5. *Ibid.,* p. 47.
6. *Ibid.,* p. 48.
7. *Ibid.,* p. 49.
8. Paul J. Franz, Jr., in a letter to the author.
9. Helen H. Couch, *op. cit.,* pp. 50, 51.
10. Henry Noble MacCracken, *The Hickory Limb* (New York: Charles Scribner's Sons, 1950), p. 190.

V   *Methods and Machinery*

Nothing comes amiss, so money comes
withal.

—*The Taming of the Shrew*

Educational fund-raising in this country has not often enough
been powered by a good case, first-rate leadership, and a
group of volunteers adequate in numbers and strong enough in
their commitment to the college or university to be effective
advocates. Of the three assets, team work most often has been
missing.

Given the basic working assets, however, what are the most
effective methods a college or university may use to raise funds
adequate to its purposes?

Until recent years most colleges, through their trustees,
have looked to the president both to develop an educational
program which on its merits would attract funds, and to go
and sell this program to the institution's constituencies.
Charles W. Eliot felt that a university president ought for the
most part to avoid such commerce; [1] but, in truth, few *college*
heads have been able to do so, for it is an inexorable demand.
Realistically, one of the first functions of an academic president is to represent his institution. He is its Lord High Everything, if anyone is; and prospects for large gifts prefer in general to discuss them with the top man.

Choices
Today, however, laying the main burden of fund-raising on
the president is antediluvian. His job has endless facets, but

his durability is not endless. Planning is the key to solving his institution's problems of getting adequate financial support. In seeking it, the president and trustees have, basically, three choices of methods:

1. Try to muddle through unaided; don't look too hard at the monster lest it be seen in its horrendous size; and hope for beneficence, from somewhere, corresponding to need. This is no method at all, and it invites disaster. A wise, long-experienced consultant, Harold J. Seymour, has observed:

> The institutions standing the best chance of [receiving] outside help are those doing the most to help themselves; by proof of full exercise of internal economies, by getting all the operating income the traffic will bear, by striving hard to reach their full potentials on annual giving, and in general using to the utmost all of the fundraising resources within their own constituencies.[2]

2. Engage outside professional counsel for systematic advising, or for a periodic "drive" to capitalize on an anniversary or some other special occasion in the life of the institution, or to meet an emergency. An intensive campaign at intervals and for specific purposes can reap large benefits. These may be only temporary, however, unless the institution makes fundraising among its total constituency a permanent administrative function, and constantly adds strength to strength.

3. Carry on steadily a development program based on a) the mission of the institution, its particular role in society, b) intelligent planning in which all of its responsible elements —trustees, president, faculty, alumni, other friends, and students—take part fully, and c) cultivation and solicitation for an appropriate educational program, on a broad scale, among all of the institution's constituencies.

Little time need be spent on the first "method" except to say that any board of trustees that uses it belongs with the ostriches. It makes the president a salesman rather than an educational leader. It is one reason why four to five years in the job now seems to be about par for the course. Obviously, all too many colleges still resort to this way of financing.

Hence there is need for the better education of boards of trustees and presidents in better ways of insuring the continued flow of funds that a healthy college or university needs for its continued growth. A board of trustees which does not regard itself merely as a custodian or caretaker will seek better ways.

The Nature of Professional Fund-Raising Counsel

Consider now the second method, the employment of outside professional counsel. Most of the firms operating today stem from fund-raising activities organized, for the first time on a large national scale, during the World War I period. The firms came into being for sound reasons. Organized financial appeals for all social and welfare institutions—including educational—required strong leadership, broad participation of volunteers, and careful planning and management if they were to succeed. No chairman of a campaign, no matter how able or devoted, could take direct charge and give as much time or fill as many roles as required. And it came to be realized that large scale fund-raising is a technical business which, to be carried on effectively and economically, has to be done on a professional basis.

Since 1919, professional fund-raising firms have helped to raise considerable sums of money for American colleges and universities. As their techniques have developed, so has their professional consciousness. In 1935 a number of the most experienced firms established The American Association of Fund-Raising Counsel, a nonprofit organization. It now has twenty-one members, and has adopted a code of fair practice.

Most of the established professional fund-raising firms offer either one or two types of service: 1) counseling in the raising of money, or 2) planning and management of fund-raising campaigns. Type 1 is advisory only. Type 2 includes the assignment of one or more men on a full time basis to work closely with the institution's representatives and volunteer laymen in an effort to meet a stated goal within a stated time at an agreed-upon cost. These professionals are certified to have adequate training and experience in campaign management.

The advisory service is more frequently employed by those institutions which already have a permanent, experienced staff in charge of an ongoing development program. Management service is usually sought by colleges and universities which either have no staff or desire to give an existing staff the training to be gained from a full-scale capital campaign. An experienced campaigner can transmit a good deal of fund-raising "know how" to a receptive staff.

The trustees and president of a college or university interested in having professional counsel manage a capital-gifts campaign for it generally ask about the methods employed, the time involved, and the costs. Firms which specialize in planning and managing such campaigns usually follow a procedure which includes:

1. *Investigation and survey,* a process of determining whether or not the college or university in question has the potentials for successful fund-raising. The process requires objectivity and fund-raising experience.

One leading firm invariably assigns a surveyor to go to the institution and thoroughly study its case, its field of potential support, and its potential working force. The survey requires five to six weeks, after which one month more is required at the home office to weigh the findings and prepare a report and recommendations for the institution. The standard fee for a survey by this firm is $2,500. Other firms are likely to quote costs running from $2,000 to $5,000, based on the amount of time required and of territory to be covered.

If the elements for a successful campaign are found lacking, the firm mentioned above does not offer its management service.

2. *Planning,* to make the most effective use of the factors of strength revealed by the survey—a strong case, influential leadership, a corps of enthusiastic workers, and a field of prospects capable of giving. This is the first task of the director assigned by the firm if the college's trustees engage it to conduct a campaign. A great deal depends upon the ability and experience of the campaign director. Supervision of his handling of the campaign by the firm's home office is usually guaranteed to the contracting college. In practice, however, the director assigned is virtually on his own once he reports to the client. The real test of his skill is management.

3. *Management,* the organization of volunteers, development of teamwork between leaders and the working force, definition of the field of support, and the plan to approach it. The professional staff assigned also budgets costs and establishes their control, determines time schedules, stimulates progress, and evaluates results of the completed campaign.

4. *Counseling* on the continuous raising of funds and the maintenance of sound public relations.

Fund-raising counsel plans, advises, assists in direction or management, endeavors to inspire and instruct, and suggests new ideas, but *does not solicit money.* Experience has taught that volunteers known to be closely identified with a college or university are its most effective solicitors. Paid canvassers are not effective, and laws in an increasing number of states are more and more curbing their activities. Fund-raising counsel like to compare their service to that of a football coach: he never carries the ball, but is expected to turn out winning teams.

On a capital-gifts campaign for a liberal arts college of medium size, one director with publicity assistance from the home office may be sufficient. The firm already alluded to charges $2,500 a month for the director's services. The cost of his travel after he has reached his post is charged to the college, as are expenses for printing, telephone and telegraph, and meetings. Other firms charge fees in the neighborhood of $750 a week, covering the services of the campaign director, supervision and home office services (library and listing, for example), and arrangement of feature events and dinners.

In a recent typical year, 1955–1956, total expenses—counsel's fee plus all other expenses—for capital-gifts campaigns conducted by the particular firm mentioned above amounted to an average of 11 per cent of the money raised. The range was from 4.6 per cent to 13.5 per cent. The amount of ground that has to be covered is a main factor. A college with a local constituency will have a low percentage cost. A college with a widespread alumni group and other constituencies may have a relatively high percentage cost.

The time involved will be determined by a number of factors, including geography (as above), availability of leaders and volunteers, state of cultivation of the total constituency, and willingness of the college's president and trustees to make the active campaign the prime business before them.

Basic Aims of Capital-Gifts Campaigns

The chief aim of the professionally managed capital-gifts campaign is to concentrate the appeal in a brief period, to conserve the time and efforts of the paid staff of the college or university, and by focusing attention on it and on its opportunities and needs, to obtain the maximum support in capital funds. The best conceived capital-gifts campaigns also look to the creation of goodwill as a basis for long-term, expanding support.

In the 1920s, with the help of fund-raising counsel, most of the independent, gift-supported colleges, universities, and preparatory schools raised large sums of money by "drives." During the depressed 1930s, fewer campaigns were ventured by institutions of higher education, and there were no such spectacular successes as in the preceding decade.

But since the end of the second global war Cornell University and Massachusetts Institute of Technology have raised $12.5 million and $25 million * respectively, by means of intensive capital-gifts campaigns. M.I.T. is currently undertaking another such campaign with an objective of $5 million in additional endowment for faculty salaries. In 1955–1956 the University of Chicago reaped approximately $33 million from a similar effort. (Members of the board of trustees led off by pledging $4 million.)

These notable successes have underscored the importance of a good case, good leadership and good teamwork, and a solid constituency or the basis for developing one. And in each instance the campaign was only part of a perennial, ongoing development program.

The Main Techniques

The main techniques of intensive campaigns for capital gifts are more or less standardized and recognizable—but not easy to master. Campaigns on a national scale call for organizational skills of a high order, and no less exacting is the work of "stating the case." Building an organization of volunteers to carry out specified assignments, cultivating the constituencies, preparing publicity materials, endeavoring to procure

---

* Between January 1, 1948, and June 30, 1951, the period of M.I.T.'s intensive development fund drive, 10,632 individuals (8 per cent nonalumni), 266 business corporations, and 34 foundations made gifts to the Institute. The total given or pledged was $25,668,532, of which about 26 per cent came from companies, 24 per cent from individuals, and 50 per cent from foundations and other sources.

advance special gifts which generally measure the success of the whole enterprise, arranging a campaign schedule that will lead constructively through the preliminary stages up to the "kick-off dinner" and into the intensive period of solicitation and the mopping-up that follows—all of these elements require time, energy, and talent.

Objectivity and the ability to make a fresh approach to the solution of a fund-raising problem are advantages which professional fund-raising counsel generally can bring to a college. Optimism and energy on the part of counsel have scored more than one victory over the timidity or inertia of presidents and trustees. Moreover, counsel has often found and exploited the elements of a good case where the client either failed to perceive them or did not know how to use them to best advantage.

Often, too, professional outside counsel has been able to suggest beneficial changes—in alumni affairs, public relations, and even trustee and presidential relations—the importance of which entrenched individuals or groups did not realize or which they resisted.

On balance, the device of the intensive capital-gifts campaign has proved to be sound in concept, well adapted to the existing circumstances, and effective in the results procured.

The Danger of Expecting Too Much

Where fund-raising counsel in its management role has not fulfilled all expectations, there has generally been a failure to understand this role in advance, or to set achievable goals. Any college or university which employs a professional fund-raising firm to manage a campaign has to realize that it is an aid, seldom effective without institutional and lay leadership. Perhaps the chief cause of less-than-par results is the mistaken belief that once an experienced individual or firm has been employed, the institution's trustees and officials can relax and leave the fund-raising to the professionals. There is no panacea, unless it be organized hard work.

In contemplating the engagement of professional assistance, trustees have to realize that the driving force comes from the institution. It is not an import. Determination to make the campaign a success springs from people who have the college or university close to their hearts.

A second cause of occasional failure to make par with a capital-gifts campaign (the chief cause, in the view of an outstanding leader among fund-raising counsel) lies in not setting the right goals. In one instance the firm consulted gave a "curbstone guess" that a certain institution could raise $2 million in capital gifts. A survey which the firm was engaged to make confirmed this judgment. The officers of the institution insisted on going after $4 million. A total of $2.1 million was actually raised, and the leaders and workers in the campaign felt frustrated, despite the fact that they had gotten a little more out of the constituency than professional counsel had predicted.

In contrast, immediately after World War II Lehigh University accepted professional counsel's advice that it go initially after $1.5 million instead of the $4 million it had in mind. After getting a real development program under way, the university repeated a capital-gifts campaign in 1954–1956. Both of these capital-gifts campaigns within a ten-year period exceeded their goals; the second one netted over $6 million. During this decade the university's total assets increased from $16.4 million to over $33 million, mostly as a result of the continuing development program.

A third reason for occasional failure is that the college or university involved may lack the strength to make a capital-gifts campaign succeed. Experience has made it clear that an intensive campaign can not greatly assist a college or university which does not already possess the three essentials of a strong case, a sound constituency, and good leadership and teamwork. An intensive campaign may help to make a strong institution stronger; it seldom can make a weak one strong. Counseling, on the other hand, can be helpful to nearly all colleges and universities. It can assist them to build up the strength needed to go after capital funds.

The Right Perspective on Capital-Gifts Campaigns

Some presidents and trustees have been led to feel that the results obtained through an intensive campaign do not basically solve an institution's money-raising problems; that it is too demanding of the energies of a few key leaders to be repeated, as almost surely it must, within a decade. Lehigh University holds an opposite view, and has an impressive record of fund-raising since 1946 to give it weight. To meet its considerable needs for capital purposes, Lehigh has had two special campaigns. To meet the need for an expanding operating budget, the university has put increased emphasis on its alumni fund and on its business and industry program.

Arnaud C. Marts, Chairman of Marts & Lundy, Inc., has said:

> It [the capital-gifts campaign] is just as inadequate for that continuous usage as the alumni fund is for nonrecurring capital needs. The campaign can be used once in five years, or seven years, or ten years, when a special effort must be made for a new building or a new professorship, which will require personal selling methods, but, in the interim, it should not be used as a substitute for the Annual Alumni Fund.[3]

That firm and the other most experienced fund-raising counsel advise strongly against any let-down, after a capital-gifts effort, in a college's program of development. To relax then is to forfeit many of the important benefits—of greater goodwill, for instance—that generally follow upon an intensive campaign ably conducted. Exploiting a centennial, for example, may require only a short term "drive" with high octane. But expert counsel urges that benefits from it, even during the low-pressure periods of the ongoing development program, are cumulative.[4]

The principle of feedback is at work here.

The concept and methods of a development program are so basic to college and university fund-raising that they will be treated separately, in Chapter VI.

Summary

The notion that the president alone is responsible and can raise adequate funds for a college or university is obsolete.

Outside professional counsel can be, and usually is, an aid. It can be engaged for a) advisory service or b) management of a capital-gifts campaign.

Advisory service is most often employed by institutions that have a continuous development program with permanent staffs.

Management service is usually sought by a college or university that has no such staff, or desires to train an existing staff in campaign methods.

These methods and the techniques employed are fairly standardized and recognizable, but difficult to master.

A capital-gifts campaign at intervals, set in the matrix of a continuous development program, can harvest large benefits that no other device brings in equally well, provided the institution has a good case, good leadership and teamwork, and a solid constituency.

Objectivity and the ability to make a fresh approach to solving its fund-raising problems are advantages which professional counsel generally can bring to a college or university.

Counsel is an *aid,* not a substitute for institutional leadership and "legwork."

A capital-gifts campaign may not succeed fully if it does not have realistic goals.

Some institutions are better aided by counseling than by management service.

REFERENCES

Chapter V

1. Morris Hadley, *Arthur Twining Hadley* (New Haven: Yale University Press, 1948), p. 127. A. T. Hadley wrote: "When it comes to obtaining funds as opposed to spending them, the duty of the president, while a most important one, is performed on rather different lines from that which is commonly supposed. President Eliot told me when I first took office that it was generally a mistake for the president of a large university to ask for money directly, except in a case where there had been a previous intimation that such a request would be welcome. He said that the duty of the president should be to have his plans in such clear shape that they would appeal to a man who was interested; and that the president's appeal was far stronger when made in the form of a plan than when made in the form of a request."

2. Harold J. Seymour, "Trends in College and University Finance and Promotion" (substance of a talk at Harvard University on March 3, 1954), p. 2.

3. Arnaud C. Marts, "Educational Philanthropy," an address delivered to District II of the American Alumni Council at Pocono Manor, Pennsylvania, January 26, 1949, pp. 23–24.

4. A brief and excellent booklet on intensive campaigning (not for higher education alone) is David M. Church, *So—You're Going to Raise Funds* (New York: National Publicity Council for Health and Welfare Services, Inc., 1957). Mr. Church is Executive Director of the American Association of Fund-Raising Counsel, Inc., and has had many years of experience in raising funds for educational and other social institutions, as well as for national projects like the U.S.O. and the National War Fund. The booklet treats preliminary factors to be considered; fundamentals of successful fund-raising; the approach; the actual operation; some final steps; and a summary of ways and means.

VI The Development Program —
Continuous Campaign

> Most agencies meet their financial difficul-
> ties as emergencies. What is needed in most
> instances is a continuous and cumulative
> program for the purpose of building suffi-
> cient capital to meet expanding needs and
> to safeguard programs at times of special
> peril.
>
> —LYMAN L. PIERCE *

Money-raising is no longer the burden of the multiple-duty
president. Neither is it a problem to be solved by a one-shot
treatment. It is a permanent problem which can be dealt with
only on a continuous basis. Hence a development program is
an inevitable part of the administrative machinery of a college
or university.

A development program that wages a continuous campaign
for financial support is today an inescapable necessity for any
college or university or specialized school which aims to remain or become strong. Funds adequate to its maintenance
and growth must be procured from all potential sources of
support, all "identifiable constituencies." This fact is as cogent
for publicly controlled institutions as for the privately controlled, which, except for income from tuition and fees, are
almost wholly gift supported.

Henry Adams a half century ago wrote, "The whole problem of education is one of its cost in money." [1] This is the
chief problem today. Various solutions which have been tried

* Lyman L. Pierce, *How to Raise Money* (New York and London:
Harper & Brothers, 1932), p. 218.

during more than three centuries of higher education in the United States all add up to the constant search—by the most systematic methods—for adequate support by the responsible officers and friends of each institution.

Acquiring Means Adequate to the Purposes

American higher education is in the best sense of the word a "growth industry." Always it should aim to grow in quality. Frequently, in response to the demands of American society, it must increase the scope of its services. Quantitatively, as today, it often has to cope with expanding enrollments. Higher education cannot with success do any of these things spasmodically or by ephemeral means.

The basic importance of a development program is that it enables a college or university to chart its growth, to anticipate emergencies, and to meet the legitimate, considered needs of all parts of the institution. Such a program of fund-raising is merely the planning and execution of a conscious, continuous effort to increase an institution's financial resources by utilizing a combination of the most effective techniques to produce results within a given period of time. The development program is grounded in the institution's broad service to the nation. It has a wider appeal than any one objective.[2]

This kind of program is winning steadily wider acceptance. It makes institutional fund-raising what in fact it has always been—a full time administrative function in a college or university. The executive officer in charge is the quarterback on a team which, in order to win, has to have many times eleven men.

Supervised by a committee of topflight trustees and alumni, the work of the development council becomes an official part of the institution rather than a problem for the volunteer alumni group. Another advantage of the council is that large donors are more likely to give to an official project of the trustees than to an unofficial activity of an independent alumni association.

The development committee of the institution's board of trustees (or governing board under whatever title) should— as at Lehigh University and at Northwestern University, for example—form the nucleus of the development council. The quality of their commitment to its principle and program naturally has much to do with the measure of its success.

The council should supervise *all* of the college or university's fund-raising.

How important it is to relate this function to the institution's educational program and opportunities rather than merely to needs is demonstrated by the fact that during the fiscal year 1954–1955 a group of twenty-three private universities received more than 30 per cent of the voluntary support accorded 728 degree-granting colleges and universities in the United States.[3] By and large, this group includes the major independent, gift-supported universities which maintain educational programs of the broadest scope and highest quality.

Skeptics might comment, "The rich shall inherit the earth." But observe the significant finding of James R. Reynolds, Assistant to the President at Harvard, one of the twenty-three universities mentioned:

Now let us consider where Harvard's capital money has come from. A study has revealed that a tiny fraction of *one percent* of the donors has given *90 percent of all the new capital* Harvard has received in the previous 20 years. This fact must have given Mr. Conant pause for thought. This study also showed that there was a distinct correlation between University activity, either in the form of campaigning or in the form of general publicity such as occurred during the Tercentenary Celebration, and the receipt by the University of bequests.

In other words, it appeared that gifts had not come to the University just by chance and that everything could not be left to chance in the future, but that Harvard should always be doing something concrete. The report laid emphasis on the thought that Harvard should make some effort to know and cultivate the larger potential donors whether they were alumni or merely friends.[4]

Organization of a Development Program

In the organization of the development program and the development council, as in its executive leadership, there is no set pattern for all colleges and universities to follow. But there is a general framework, both for the policy and plans group and for the operating committees, which ordinarily takes a form something like this:

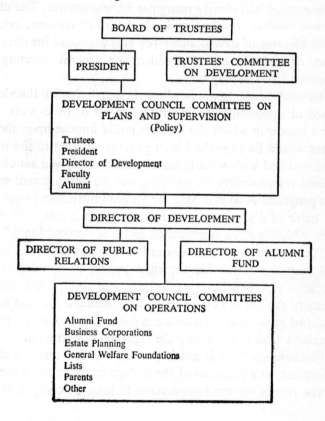

It may be repeated that representation of key trustees on the development council is of high importance. Also important is the choice of the executive officer in charge of the functioning of the program. He is its Atlas, and has to be placed in the firmest position possible. This person and his job belong in the institution's uppermost scale of affairs. The man or woman in the post is an executive working with the board of trustees.

At its peril an institution will underrate or downgrade this position. The trustees have the obligation to set up the job as strongly as they can, so that both the institution itself as well as its publics will clearly recognize its importance. The chain of responsibility, originating in the board of trustees, extends to the director of development (or vice president for development, or assistant to the president, or general secretary, or whatever his title may be).

His work is not "spare part" work, but basic, full time labor aimed at upbuilding the institution in all of its aspects. The worst handicap which the trustees could impose upon the director would be to make him a general assistant to the president, saddled with a portfolio of duties and given no clearly defined responsibility for carrying out the development council's program. Also it is easy for an administration to get into the habit of diverting the director, without intent, into other work which is often rationalized as being "promotional."

The trustees may not—indeed it is likely they will not—find easy the search for the right person to appoint to this executive position. He is a relatively new species, the requirements of the job are exacting, and the demand for competent, qualified personnel exceeds the supply. Even so, a few guidelines may lead to recruiting the right man or woman.

Fundamentally, it is not important that the director of development be a graduate of the college or university which he serves. It is of the most importance to take the competent man where he can be found. In the second place, the trustees and president should look for a person who has these basic qualifications: a genuine interest in education, a talent for organization and teamwork, promotional ability, a good sense of public relations values, ability to take the initiative, unlimited energy, and (unless his staff is to include one or more scriveners) skill in writing clear and effective English. Previous experience in fund-raising is not essential.

It is illuminating and helpful to consider where a number of leading colleges and universities have found executive officers for their development programs, and the kinds of work which they had done previously. The University of Michigan, the University of Pennsylvania, and others have former members of fund-raising agencies in charge of their development programs. But this type of personnel is not available in large numbers.

Other representative institutions have entrusted the executive leadership of their development programs to people of varied backgrounds, as for example: Carleton College, a former magazine official; Colby College, a former insurance executive; Colgate University, a professor of education, an alumnus, from its own faculty; Occidental College, a retired (but vigorous) business executive; Ohio State University, a lawyer and alumnus; Rensselaer Polytechnic Institute, a former faculty member and director of public relations; Vassar, a professor of Greek from its own faculty; Wellesley, an alumna with promotional experience who had been with a large Boston department store; and Yale, a graduate who had been in the investment security business.

No single pattern, but all excellent people and able operators!

Structure

Colleges and universities which have well knit, responsive

constituencies tend to get along best with a core group—policy committee, central committee, steering committee, or what you will—compact in numbers and centered closely around the chief administrative officers of the institution. Others, usually including the larger institutions but not these alone, will often be found to have as many as twenty-five or thirty members of this policy commitee. Included in this number will be found the nucleus for each of the working committees, into which they lead naturally and with an eye to which it is well to select them.

In this group will generally be included trustees, administrative officers, faculty members, alumni, leaders from business and industry, and perhaps even parents. All of these groups have a large stake in the college or university. All should be able to contribute to its leadership.

Since the basic purpose of the development council is to undergird the institution's educational program with adequate financial means, the council's job is to inform and to cultivate the various parts of the total constituency and in turn to solicit them. There follows a need for subcommittees, as many as may be deemed necessary and each with a chairman selected from the policy committee, to work actively in seeking:

1. Annual gifts through the alumni fund.

2. Gifts from parents (those of members now in or recently graduated from college).

3. Gifts from corporations in business and industry.

4. Gifts from alumni and other special friends for capital purposes: special endowments (as of professorships), building funds for special schools, or memorials, for example.

5. Bequests and annuities.

6. Foundation grants.

7. Research funds, through foundations or through business and industrial corporations.

8. Gifts and grants from all other potential sources among the "identifiable constituencies."

The size of each subcommittee will naturally be determined by the scope of the job to be done, and by the number of qualified workers who can be enlisted. At one time Cornell University's committee on bequests and annuities in the Cornellian Council inclued more than 800 Cornell lawyers scattered throughout the United States and all over the world. But it is impossible to expect any such number of volunteers to be self-starters, or, once started, to proceed on their own power without the constant supply of spark from headquarters. In time Cornell found that this number of lawyers was unwieldy, and it has reduced the size of its committee on bequests and annuities. Wellesley has a bequest committee of twenty-five lawyers, under the chairmanship of a trustee of the College.

Functioning of the Council

Nearly all of the large gift-supported universities, and many of the state universities and independent colleges as well, have adopted or are adopting the development program, shaping it to their own needs. A glance at the attached chart underscores some well established facts and indicates a number of natural variations. In a majority of instances the executive officer of the council or fund gives 100 per cent of his time to the job of making it function. That is as it should be. Also, he has to have on his team an office staff able to carry heavy and varied burdens.

Even more important, the director of development requires the guidance and co-operation of the policy-making council itself, ranging in numbers from the cohesive core group of nine members, as at Dartmouth, up to the 400 elected volunteers in the Stanford University Associates. Like Cornell University's development council of 750 members, this group obviously includes "eyes and ears" as well as guiding minds—

which can hardly, lest there be confused counsels and divided authority, exceed thirty in number.

Soliciting committees are generally about six in number, and the total of their active members may run as high as 2,600, as at the University of Pennsylvania. On the sound principle that a development council asks a number of people to accept a part of the burden of its work but overloads none of them, few colleges have difficulty in enlisting volunteers for the varied work of the council.

In order to facilitate its work, an institution must produce and have available for distribution printed materials which set forth its needs. Thereafter it is even more important to have college officers or other members of the development council make personal calls on key prospects. Working out the right assignments and seeing tactfully that they are carried out is one of the director's chief responsibilities, for the principal way by which most colleges can get money is relentlessly to ask for it, year in and year out.

While laying emphasis on the annual, unremitting search for gifts, which is of course the fundamental purpose and the main virtue of the development program, most institutions include within the framework of the council a provision for intensive capital-gifts campaigns if and when necessary. This is the wise course. It is to be observed that the successful capital gifts appeals made since 1945 by the University of Chicago, Cornell University, and Massachusetts Institute of Technology were merely parts of long range funding plans that will be carried on steadily for the development of those institutions.

Weaknesses appear, of course, in this as in any other kind of fund-raising machinery, but are easier to get at and deal with. Yet in spite of limitations of budget, or the lack of more extensive publicity or of more volunteers, for instance, most development programs appear to be accomplishing their basic purposes and to be getting results which are satisfactory to the boards of trustees concerned.

Most of them obviously realize that in order to get money, through this or any other means, it is necessary to spend money. The trustees of the institution (among the number indicated in the chart) whose development program cost $448,000 to operate in the last fiscal year undoubtedly feel that the more than $22 million which the program brought in during the year represents a gratifying return. The expense of operation was 2 per cent.

Most development programs, as they should, include the alumni (annual) fund. For this holds the key to the whole money-raising program of an institution of higher education. The funds which it garners in a year's time are in themselves increasingly important to tightly budgeted colleges and universities.

Above and beyond this is the demonstrated fact that the annual fund, which forms in most contributors the gratifying habit of regular giving to income, is a feed line for capital benefactions. Several leading universities have in recent times suspended the annual fund while conducting intensive campaigns for capital gifts, and feel that it was a mistake to do so. "Giving made easy," through the annual fund, is valuable for itself and in no way interferes with the occasional search for capital gifts for special purposes. Indeed, it is the best possible base on which to build for future large contributions, and all the while it produces steady annual income which no college can afford to waive.

These considerations have influenced and shaped two of our most productive development programs, those at Wellesley and at Yale. Each merits close inspection, which reveals facts having a wide applicability.

Name of Institution	1. Council Founded	2. Central Responsibility	3. In Charge	4. Time Devoted	5. Office Staff	6. Alumni Fund Included?	7. Size of Council	8. Number of Meetings Each Year
AMHERST COLLEGE	1951	Trustees' Committee on Endow't.	Committee Chairman	Voluntary	3 plus	No	21	2
CARLETON COLLEGE	1948	Board of Trustees	V-P	100%	13 full time	Yes	121	Numerous
COLBY COLLEGE	1952	Board of Trustees	Dir. of Dev.	100%	6	No	12	11
CORNELL UNIVERSITY	1948	Board of Trustees	V-P	100%	11	Yes	750	Advisory Board 4 times
DARTMOUTH COLLEGE	1949	Board of Trustees	Dir. of Dev.	100%	22	Yes	9	Varies
NORTH- WESTERN UNIVERSITY	1926	Board of Trustees	Dir. of Dev.	100%	34	Yes	14	4
UNIVERSITY OF NOTRE DAME	1947	President	Dir., N.D. Fndn.	100%	10	Yes	10	Often
OHIO STATE UNIVERSITY	1939	Board of Trustees	Exec. Dir.	50%	12	Yes	10	2 and on call
UNIVERSITY OF PENNSYLVANIA	1924	President	V-P	70%	40	Yes	14	4
RENSSELAER POLYTECHNIC INSTITUTE	1953	Board of Trustees	General Secretary	100%	3	No	17	3
STANFORD UNIVERSITY	1936	Board of Trustees	General Secretary	100%	35	Yes	400	11
SWARTHMORE COLLEGE	1950	Trustees, & Alumni Exec. Comm.	V-P	50%	3	Yes	14	2
WELLESLEY COLLEGE	1950	Trustees Develop. Fund Comm.	Dir. of Dev. Fund.	100%	10	Yes	11	3
YALE UNIVERSITY	1947	Yale Corp'n.	Asst. to Pres.	100%	5	No	81	2

9. Who Chair Committees?	10. Number of Committees	11. Total Members	12. Any Trouble Enlisting?	13. Capital-Gifts Campaigns?	14 If Not, Why?	15. Adequate Results?	16. Weaknesses?
Committee members	6	21	No	Plan none	Favor continuous effort	—— ·	No one devoting full time
Council members	——	——	On contrary	Yes		Yes	——
Council Chairman	4	28	No	Yes	——		——
Development Council members	5	125	No	Yes		Yes	——
Committee Chairmen	3	15 approx.	No	Yes	——	——	——
Trustee members	5	150	No	Yes	——		——
——		212	——	Yes	——	Yes	Could use more area manpower
Fund Board members	2	5	No	Yes	——		Not geared for proper publicity
Three Trustees, 10 alumni, 2 non-alumni	17	2643	No	Yes	——		Too many U. of P. campaigns going on simultaneously
Development Council members	11	350	No	No	Favor continuous effort	Yes	Need even more active volunteer participation
Development Council members	7	148	No	Yes	——	Yes and No	Need even more active volunteer participation
Development Council members	——	——	No	Yes	——	Yes	——
Fund Committee Chairman	3	41	Rarely	Yes	——	Yes	
Pres. of Dev. Council	2	81	No	Yes	——	Yes	——

But first a look at the development experience of three other varied institutions, in alphabetical order, which also have planned their financial growth carefully.

Carleton College

The basic importance of a development program is well demonstrated by Carleton—co-educational, with 900 to 1,000 students, and located in the middle west. As far back as 1930 the college carefully defined its objectives at nearly $11.1 million.[5] Moreover, Carleton defined the sources from which this money would have to be procured. The public, it said, rather than the students, must provide the physical plant and endowment funds, as well as current funds to take care of about 45 per cent of the expenditures for educational purposes. Additional funds would also be sought for scholarships, both endowed and current, and for revolving student-loan funds.

This was a major undertaking. It required many new sources of gifts. Thus in 1941 an alumni fund with a full time director was established, and in 1948 the position of vice president in charge of public relations and fund-raising was created. Since then a full time news bureau director has been employed, and the editor of college publications put on a full time basis. These individuals, together with the alumni director and their staffs, are all responsible to the vice president.

This expanded development staff has assisted the president in expanding the sources of gifts to the college. During the last decade 25,000 gifts totaling $516,000 have been given to Carleton by the alumni alone. This total represents an increase of 454 per cent in the number and 400 per cent in the amount, compared to the decade 1936–1945. Gifts from parents of present and former students who are not themselves alumni of Carleton have increased from about $20,000 in 1945 to an average of $213,000 for the last three years.

But spreading the base has been only part of the story.

Individual gifts have been on as high a scale as at any time in Carleton's history. In 1952 an anonymous donor pledged stocks valued at $1 million as endowment for a new library, provided $1.5 million could be raised in bona fide subscriptions in two years for the building itself. By 1954 the $1.5 million had been subscribed by only 250 donors, and 10 per cent gave 90 per cent of the total. By that time the original $1 million in securities for endowment had increased in value to $1,313,038, making a grand total for the project of $2.8 million—the largest gift in Carleton's history.

The effectiveness of the college's development program is measured by the fact that its total assets have grown in value from $4,135,428 in 1928 to $12,022,081 in 1957.

Colby College

Although in size and situation it is at the other extreme from Northwestern and Yale (which will be considered presently), Colby College also shows strikingly what can be accomplished through a development program. Colby, founded in 1813, is a co-educational college located in central Maine, with around 1,200 students, who come mostly from New England and the Middle Atlantic states. Its alumni in general are not well-to-do, and the college does not have the wealth of any metropolis at its door. Yet, by steadily employing development techniques, Colby has achieved remarkable results.

In 1929 a state-sponsored survey made by outside experts of the four senior colleges and universities in Maine pointed out that on its old campus by the Kennebec River, where it had given its first instruction in 1818, Colby was certain to languish. Industrial Waterville had in fact overflowed the college, and its further development on its old river-and-railroad-bound campus was impossible.

In 1930 the president and trustees decided to move "when feasible." An Augusta philanthropist offered protected land in the state capital, twenty miles to the south. But the townspeople of Waterville countered by subscribing, in one of the blackest years of the depression, $100,000 to purchase for the college 650 acres of land on Mayflower Hill, two miles west of the old campus located in the northern part of the city. Colby they considered their one "depression-proof industry."

Then by successive steps the college laid the ground for what has become a full scale development program. In 1937 a memorial chapel was constructed with funds given by an alumnus; and then, after being primed by professional counsel, the college trustees, faculty, alumni, and other friends pushed through limited-objective campaigns for a men's union building and another for women. In 1939–1940 Colby made an intensive appeal for the "Maine Million" with which to carry on its total development, and in 1948–1951 the college by its own efforts raised slightly more than $2 million in the Mayflower Hill Development Fund campaign.

At the outset there was no single large benefaction (as at Duke and at Wake Forest) to insure Colby's safe transit up Mayflower Hill, and doubters called the bold enterprise "Johnson's folly." The late President Franklin W. Johnson, who retired in 1942, lived to see his "venture of faith" come true. With unflagging energy and courage, he was accustomed to say in the face of all discouragements, "What must be done can be done."

The central direction and drive for these various Colby appeals has come from the board of trustees (including the president) and the alumni. Central organization of the development program was begun in 1936 when the fund council was created. Also since that year Colby has had an assistant to the president who has concentrated on cultivation and solicitation of prospects, many of them non-alumni, all over the United States. Results from this agency work or "retail selling" have been excellent.

The executive personnel managing the day-in-day-out work

at the college has included in turn the alumni secretary, the director of public relations, and the vice president, who under Colby's by-laws is now responsible for its financial affairs, including fund-raising. In 1952 several basic factors resulted in the change of name of the fund-raising team to the Colby College Development Council, with a director of development as its executive officer. The college makes him completely responsible for the management of the council.

In 1953 Colby carefully weighed its needs, some of them new and some for physical units which had been included in the architect's original designs for a functional campus to house 1,000 students. The college determined on a $6 million program for the next decade, confident of carrying it successfully to completion because it now possesses the "know how" and also because Colby has steadily kept its valid goals and its needs and opportunities clear in the eyes of its total constituency.

Colby's constituency deserves notice. Approximately 14,-000 individual contributors and a large number of business corporations have helped Colby to overcome the handicaps of depression, two wars, and inflation, and to make good its "venture of faith." It is of particular interest that one-half of the individual contributors are not alumni of the college.

The comparative summary of Colby's achievements through its development program is inspiring:

	1930	1957
Students	605	1,156
Faculty	37	98
Buildings	18	24
		(all new)
Volumes in library	70,000	181,000
Annual budget	$285,000	$1,879,000
Endowment	$1,465,000	$6,764,000
Investment in educational plant	$1,045,000	$7,761,000
Total assets	$2,700,000	$16,134,000

Dartmouth College

Dartmouth—as far as Colby from the country's main financial and industrial centers—also has developed outreach in order to produce intake. The college was 125 years old before it began a systematic cultivation of its constituencies. William Jewett Tucker, President of Dartmouth from 1893 to 1909, laid the basis for today's fruitful work of the development council. Dr. Tucker saw that the college's sources of support were 1) its own earning power, which had to be used to the fullest extent, 2) its alumni, and 3) its other friends.

At the outset Dr. Tucker had to repair the college's relations with its alumni. He fostered the founding of more alumni clubs, and was tireless in visiting them to explain the work and aspirations of the college. He succeeded in generating in them a sense of pride and affiliation. It was to serve Dartmouth well.

A fire actually touched off the series of events which led to the formation, in 1906, of an annual giving program. In February 1904, Dartmouth Hall, which for more than 100 years had been the central point of the life of the college, burned to the ground. At once a group of potent alumni in Boston began making plans for a mass meeting of alumni to consider how to raise funds for rebuilding Old Dartmouth. The letter which announced the meeting opened with the sentence: "This is not an invitation; it is a summons."

The alumni responded vigorously. Within two years, $240,000 had been raised—enough to rebuild Old Dartmouth and to build an auditorium as well, for which an appeal several years earlier had failed.

With momentum up, Dartmouth made annual giving the basis of its remarkably successful alumni fund, which dates from 1915. Its fundamental purpose was and is to supply unrestricted funds in order to meet current operating expenses, and to make possible a quality of educational program which the college's endowments could not conceivably support.

The value of this "living endowment" shows in the record. In 1915 the Dartmouth Alumni Fund raised $6,580 for the college; in 1957 it raised $928,592.

For years the Dartmouth Alumni Fund fared so well that little emphasis was given to the search for capital gifts. There was some fear, moreover, that capital-gifts campaigns might jeopardize the alumni fund. As a matter of record, Dartmouth conducted no such campaign during the presidency of Ernest Martin Hopkins, 1916 to 1945. His viewpoint is interesting:

My own belief, and the conviction which has made me now for nearly twenty years oppose every suggestion of a capital fund drive for Dartmouth, is that so far as alumni support goes I am perfectly willing to have the alumni keep the principal in their own possession if they will give us the income. A college only rarely secures, under any circumstances, a gift where the principal can be used, and for the great run of alumni I think that a man will pay the interest on a larger amount than he is ready to capitalize at any given time during his lifetime. Meanwhile, the alumnus of large means who is disposed to make a gift of major dimensions to become endowment principal is far more inclined to do so, in my belief, if he has come to a realization and understanding of college needs gradually, through the campaigns which attend the alumni fund subscriptions.[6]

Not until 1937 was any major addition made to Dartmouth's fund-raising program. Then the classes of 1913 and 1914 determined to make gifts to the college of endowment funds on the occasions of their twenty-fifth reunions. They undertook to set a pattern of such endowment fund gifts, with the income unrestricted as to use. The plan succeeded. The Class of 1923 gave the college $107,000 at its "twenty-fifth" in 1948, since which time $100,000 has been par for the course. The total of these class gifts to endowment is now more than $1.5 million—an amount given in addition to what these same classes have contributed annually through the alumni fund.

On one occasion since World War II, Dartmouth sought about $4 million for a new auditorium and associated projects. This sole capital-fund appeal did not succeed. The college then realized the need for a comprehensive plan to raise funds for future development, and for the manpower and experience to make the plan effective. Hence the Dartmouth Development Council was formed. It has a membership of seventeen: two representatives of the general alumni body, one faculty member, one trustee, one non-alumnus, and, ex-officio, the president of the alumni council, the chairmen of the alumni fund committee, the memorial fund committee, and the bequest committee; the secretary, treasurer, and provost of the college, a representative of the trustees' planning committee, the deans of the three associated schools, and one representative of the student body.

The Dartmouth Trustees' Committee on Development (planning) determines top policy on all fund-raising for the college, and the development council is advisory to the committee.

Dartmouth has confirmed the alumni fund as the keystone to its whole fund-raising structure—the element to which each alumnus owes a first responsibility. The fund continues to be a "budgeted asset" for current operations. By way of capital, the class memorial funds have been confirmed as the responsibility of those classes which have yet to come up to their "twenty-fifth." As a counterpart for classes more than twenty-five years out of college, a bequest program has been instituted.

Other parts of Dartmouth's development program call for active efforts to gain all possible support from foundations, business corporations, and friends, as well as for specialized solicitations of individuals or groups whose interests in the projects concerned made it wise to seek *inter vivos* gifts beyond what they might normally give through other established parts of the development program.

The bequest and estate planning program (which will be described in a later chapter) has been the most successful new element in the comprehensive plan.[7]

To make it fully effective in meeting Dartmouth's responsibilities today, the college announced in January 1957 a large scale design calling for at least $25 million in new capital, and an increase of $3 million in annual income within twelve years. Plant improvements and increased faculty salaries are foremost among the needs to be met in an initial two-year intensive campaign. President John Sloan Dickey announced that Dartmouth was building up "durable strength" through increased endowment, and that "we have never had a comprehensive capital gifts campaign, and we have had no major plant gifts during the past quarter century."

Northwestern University

In 1923–1924 Northwestern University had a successful intensive campaign for capital gifts which was conducted with the assistance of professional counsel. That fund-raising effort created the momentum for the establishment of a long-range program of cultivation for gifts and bequests. Setting forth its educational goals in positive terms, the university undertook to win the support of a small but exceedingly wealthy group of prospective donors. The wisdom of this course has been borne out by results. From 1920 to 1950 the university was the beneficiary of $92 million in gifts and bequests, of which more than $60 million came from six donors.

Although persons capable of making multi-million-dollar gifts and bequests are now a diminishing breed, Northwestern University has continued to develop strength out of strength. Today a thirteen-man committee of the board of trustees is responsible for the planning and direction of all fund-raising activities of the university. Under the direction of this committee there has been established a department of development with the mission of coordinating long range needs with a vigorous program of information, cultivation, and solicitation. Included within the department under supervision of the director of development are: the offices of alumni, corporation, and foundation relations; the bequests and special gifts program; the offices of information services and program activities; and the maintenance of the gift record and addressograph departments.

One other aspect of Northwestern holds particular interest —the Northwestern University Associates. This rather elite group was established by the board of trustees in 1929, and is under the leadership of a senior trustee. In its membership are included 300 men from outside the alumni group. Its objective is simply and practically to interest influential non-alumni in Northwestern University. A series of carefully planned luncheon meetings brings the associates together frequently to hear outstanding speakers in various fields of education and science who are members of the university faculty. Although the subject of fund-raising is never introduced into these luncheon meetings, many of the university's largest gifts have come to it through the interest and activities of the associates.

More recently Northwestern has pioneered with another successful organization, the John Evans Club, founded in 1954. Named after the principal founder of the University, the club is composed of outstanding alumni. The organization receives coordination and assistance from the department of alumni relations. Criteria for membership include evidence of sustained interest in the university and the pledge to make a contribution of $10,000 or more over a ten-year period. The interest of the members is maintained through a series of meetings and special events including luncheons, dinners at the president's home, a pre-football season meeting, and a breakfast on Alumni Day. Membership has grown steadily and is now well over 100. The collective giving record during the first three years has been far in excess of the $10,000 agreed upon by each member.

The committee on development provides trustee supervision of all fund-raising programs at Northwestern. Special committees are appointed in charge of specific fund efforts, and all such committees include trustees. As an example, the chairman and vice chairman of the 1951 Centennial Campaign, as well as most of the campaign committee and the chairman of the Northwestern University Associates, were trustees and members of the committee on development.

Most gratifyingly, this development organization has "paid off" handsomely. During the first seven years of the present decade, the university has received a total in gifts from all sources in the amount of $44 million.

Wellesley College

In 1950 Wellesley's trustees and alumnae association board agreed on a consolidation of fund-raising for the college. The Wellesley College Development Fund became the inclusive channel for all gifts—from alumnae and non-alumnae, and in the form of annual contributions, capital gifts, and bequests. In the fiscal year ending June 30, 1956, Wellesley raised from all sources a total of $3,714,324; and much of this money came from alumnae who, kept aware of the needs of the college, had acquired the habit of giving.

Wellesley has an unusually cohesive group of alumnae, who form the eyes and ears as well as the persuasive voices of its National Development Fund Committee. At its core there is a policy committee of eleven members, six of whom are off campus and the other five of whom are the president, executive vice president, director of publicity, assistant to the president, and the director of the development fund. This committee, whose functioning is subject to the approval of the college's board of trustees, meets three times a year.

As already reported, Wellesley has a bequest committee of twenty-five lawyers. It has also a memorial committee of two members. Beyond these two compact committees, the college's fund organization consists of volunteer workers who act for the fund in one of three capacities: 1) 35 regional directors in charge of geographical regions, in some cases including more than one state, 2) 154 district chairmen who handle fund matters in their own limited geographical areas, working under the general supervision of their regional director, and 3) 67 class representatives who are responsible for fostering interest in the college among their classmates.

By searching for capital gifts to the development fund on an individual basis, Wellesley hopes to be able to avoid intensive capital-gifts campaigns. A bright beacon is the fact that Wellesley alumnae generally are responding well to the college's basic idea of annual, proportionate giving.

Yale University

Yale, in many ways *sui generis* in the business of raising money, which it often has raised to the level of an art, has a longer record of it than Wellesley, and yet their experiences touch at a number of points. The Yale Alumni Fund, established in 1890, was the first of its kind. But in 1947 there was  created the office of university development, with a well known faculty member, Dr. Howard W. Haggard, as director. In 1948 he acquired an assistant and in 1950 resumed teaching, leaving to his former aide the direction of the office.

In turn the university appointed an assistant to the president, who is really the vice president in charge of all the resources that Yale does not possess but hopes to acquire; and, for that purpose, the director of the office of university development is in effect his "office." The staff is of modest size: the director, an associate, and three helpers.

But this Office does not include the alumni fund, described by a recent president of Harvard as "Yale's greatest asset," although the two operations complement each other and the staffs concerned work closely together. In addition, the office of university development functions in close harmony with the alumni board, with which it helps to "service" local Yale meetings all over the country. Chiefly it makes available information about the university's current needs, and occasionally speakers.

After the office of university development had been in operation for eight years, the Yale Corporation in 1955 redefined the university's fund-raising policies to provide:

1. No all-out endowment campaign such as that of 1926–1927 which netted $20 million.

2. Further increased emphasis on the alumni fund and the bequest program.

3. Further increased emphasis on "spreading the Yale gospel"—the primary responsibility of the Yale Development Committee (special gifts.)

4. Occasional campaigns for limited objectives, such as helped to build a new wing for the art gallery, the science laboratories, and the new electrical engineering laboratory.

Yale's major aim was to protect and further develop the alumni fund, which in the fiscal year 1956–1957 brought in nearly $1.75 million and exceeded the $1 million mark for the seventh consecutive year. Also, the university had reason to believe that it could develop special gifts and bequests to the point of helping to meet some of its capital needs. It preferred to avoid the risks and disadvantages of an all-out effort by everyone in and out of the university over a two-year to three-year period, during which the diversions from educational matters would certainly represent a high cost.

As a matter of studied policy, Yale's entire fund-raising team works on a low-pressure basis.

The most interesting of the university's policy decisions

mentioned above is No. 3, affecting special gifts. Formerly the office of university development had local development committees in about sixty principal cities where there were strong, organized Yale alumni groups. Theoretically, they were supposed to screen their alumni, select the more affluent, and solicit special gifts. These committees were to be serviced and followed-up by the development office in New Haven.

For a variety of reasons the program bogged down. Yale learned from the experience, and created a development committee, limited in numbers but potent in leadership. Its job was to be cultivation, not solicitation; to disseminate the story of Yale's educational program, and to focus on it the special interests of alumni who could make special gifts for its development. There was sound reason behind the university's policy decision to revamp the development committee. In 1955–1956, while the alumni fund netted Yale $1.6 million in contributions from 30,000 alumni, 360 of these same donors made special gifts amounting to $2.92 million. So the aim of the new development committee is to educate alumni of means so that they will put Yale in their annual philanthropic budget for a special gift.

The assistant to the president explains, "Our philosophy is based on the simple premise that an informed constituency is likely to be a generous one."

Currently Yale's special gifts committee has about eighty members. Their first job was to acquire a thorough knowledge of Yale's aims and achievements. It was the responsibility of the office of university development to provide this knowledge; the job of the committee to absorb it and disseminate it to others. The functioning of the special gifts committee is aided by periodic visits of the office of university development staff personnel to members of the committee.

Each member of the committee selects eight to ten top prospects for cultivation, as in New York City; or "the top 10 per cent" in cities of less size and complexity.

Yale reports that organizing the work of its development (special gifts) committee on this basis is "one of the smartest things we have done." Its "charge" to committee members suggests the reason:

We want you to understand the *nature* of a University—the fact that we are in the *charity business,* that our needs are unending and never satisfied, and that if the time ever comes when we *don't* have a long list of things we'd like to do, you can be sure we're slipping. For a university needs to keep its plant and its products up to date just as much as General Motors or DuPont, and pleas for money to do this are healthy signs—not evidences of weakness or bad management. As your first assignment, please read it carefully—and when you next see one of your "top 10 per cent," urge him to read it too.[8]

The existence of this special gifts committee and the entire development program explains in good part a news story which appeared in *The New York Times* on October 4, 1957. The Yale University Council recommended to the Yale Corporation a ten-year program requiring a minimum of $109,-745,000 for 1) plant and equipment and 2) teaching and research. The council unanimously agreed that substantially increased faculty salaries are a "need which takes precedence over all others." But the council decided that a salary study "is properly the province of the University corporation and administrative officers."

Other Development Achievements

Another useful way of demonstrating the effectiveness of a well conceived development program is to show it at work, year after year, in three other representative colleges and universities. It will be observed that the benefits are cumulative.*

* The information given here was furnished to the author by the institutions concerned, and is used with their permission.

DAVIDSON COLLEGE

Year	Capital Gifts	Alumni Fund	Total for Year
1946–47	$ 106,168.00	$ 28,980.25	$ 135,148.25
1947–48	596,469.00	30,666.30	627,135.30
1948–49	472,966.00	29,120.96	502,086.96
1949–50	1,114,629.00 (campaign)	23,513.50	1,138,142.50
1950–51	649,667.00	50,586.96	700,253.96
1951–52	529,042.00	54,236.84	583,278.84
1952–53	828,394.00 (campaign)	61,463.70	889,857.70
1953–54	652,826.00	70,343.68	723,169.68
1954–55	481,400.00	81,739.77	563,139.77
1955–56	698,170.00	116,080.00	814,250.00
1956–57	946,854.00	125,031.00	1,171,885.00

Total Assets

Year	Buildings (Plant Fund)	Endowment	Total
1947	$2,581,992	$4,473,114	$ 7,055,106
1957	5,446,341	8,579,182	14,025,523

FRANKLIN AND MARSHALL COLLEGE

Average of gifts, including bequests, for 10 years previous to 1946 .... $ 60,000

Alumni fund of 1945 (included in average above) 8,802

1946–48 intensive campaign (Goal $600,000). Raised 854,000

The development program was started in 1951–52, and its record since then has been:

Year	Alumni Giving	Gifts from Other Sources, Current Operations	Bequests	Other Gifts, Not Including Bequests	Total
1951–52	$ 55,000	$54,000	—	$ 34,851	$144,710
1952–53	60,000	55,000	—	299,932	344,932
1953–54	143,987	45,227	$117,250	11,298	317,762
		(new president)			
1954–55	145,541	60,529	70,500	5,750	282,320
	(president and director of development resigned)				
1955–56	114,649	43,000	6,108	32,129	195,886
	(new president, new director of development)				
1956–57	Intensive campaign (goal $1,500,000).				
	Raised to date				$1,100,000

LEHIGH UNIVERSITY

The average of gifts (not including bequests) for 10 years previous to 1947 was		$ 99,307

The largest total for one year was $250,722, of which $107,000 was actually a gift to an intensive campaign then about to begin.

1947–49	Intensive campaign (goal $1,500,000). Raised	$2,000,000
1950–51	Development program initiated.	
	Gifts to alumni fund (not included under development program totals)	$ 73,059
	Other gifts, not including bequests or payments on pledges	219,240
	Total	292,299
1951–52	Full development program in action.	
	Gifts through alumni fund (now included in program)............	$ 151,348
	Other gifts (not including bequests) .	232,743
	Total	384,091
1952–53	Gifts through alumni fund	$ 201,000
	Other gifts (not including bequests of $125,005)	340,000
	Total	541,000
1953–54	Gifts through alumni fund	$ 254,508
	Other gifts (not including bequests of $71,346)	594,354
	Total	848,862
1954–56	Intensive campaign (goal $2,200,000). Raised	$2,680,878
	Other gifts (not including bequests of $1,756,953)	1,666,764
	Total	4,347,642
1956–57	Alumni annual fund	$ 358,128
	Other gifts (not including bequests of $119,324)	1,364,636
	Total	1,722,636

After several years of operation, the development program began to produce five times as much as the average for the previous ten years (without including bequests, several of which were written during the campaign). By the end of June

1956, total assets of Lehigh University had increased in ten years from $16,403,000 to $33,450,000—more than double.

Also it is of interest that numerous tax-supported universities now have established development programs. State legislatures ordinarily do not appropriate funds for certain educational activities which may mean the difference between a good institution and an excellent one. Hence the University of Mississippi has the right slogan: "University Development Is a Job for All."

The Western Conference universities all have well staffed development programs in force. That at the Ohio State University in the fiscal year 1956 brought in $800,144 from 25,-254 donors—$250,861 from 23,783 alumni. Since the development fund was organized in 1939 it has raised more than $6.5 million. The fact that its alumni and other individual friends give the university *voluntary* support has had the effect of causing the Ohio state legislature to be increasingly liberal in its appropriations to Ohio State.

This same kind of report comes from other state universities which have set up development programs.

Money, Money, Money

It bears repeating that in order to raise money a college has to spend money. Contributions must be gotten; as Harvard has demonstrated, they do not merely flow in. Tight budgets and the salient need to apply all possible funds to depressed faculty salary schedules make presidents and trustees look with a calculating eye on money required to conduct a development program.

Here are a few operating records to consider.

In 1952 the Director for Funds of the American Alumni Council made a survey of fund-raising costs among member institutions. He reported:

As expected, the cost-of-operation question was a difficult one for many to answer, since costs are so tied up with those of the alumni association and other programs. A clear cut answer is often impossible, we realized, but enough were received to form the basis for some general conclusions. Among those reporting, the cost of operation per dollar raised ranged from a low of 3¢ to a high of 49¢. The average was 13¢.[9]

This statement needs some explanation. Invariably the funds with the high cost per dollar raised were ones just getting started. Naturally they could expect heavy promotion costs before raising much money. The Director of Funds questioned cost per dollar raised as low as three cents because he doubted that these funds reported all of the costs of operation. He concluded that a fair average was somewhere around ten to fifteen cents per dollar raised.

In the chart attached to this chapter, data are given on the development programs of fourteen institutions of higher education. Ten reported on their costs of operations during the last fiscal year, and the averages are as follows:

	Average
Six universities	$261,165
Three colleges	79,923
Ten institutions, including one technological	197,657

All of the ten institutions reported their totals of voluntary gifts received, from all sources, in the 1957 survey of voluntary support for higher education, conducted jointly by the American Alumni Council, the American College Public Relations Association, and the Council for Financial Aid to Education. Their receipts and costs were as follows:

Group	*Grand Total of Gifts Received*	*Total Operating Costs of Development Program*	*Percentage Cost per Dollar Raised*
Six universities	$81,990,155	$1,566,988	1.91 per cent
Three colleges	9,157,124	239,770	2.61 per cent
Ten institutions	94,102,803	1,956,569	2.10 per cent

These figures need slight interpretation. One university was conducting a capital-gifts campaign within the framework of the development program during the fiscal year, and special expenses charged to that account lifted this institution's percentage cost per dollar raised above the group average. On the other hand, one of the three colleges, with a development fund office not yet fully organized, had an unusually low percentage cost per dollar raised.

Also, it is true, all ten of the institutions represented in the table above are veterans in the raising of voluntary support. Their promotional costs are probably low, and the level of their voluntary assistance high. Nonetheless, taken as they are, the figures provide convincing evidence of the relative inexpensiveness of a continuous development program; of the fact that it is necessary to spend money in order to get money; and of the fact that sizeable sums of money can be gotten for a college, year in and year out.

Summary

A development program that wages a continuous campaign for financial support is today an inescapable necessity for any college or university which aims to remain or become strong.

The basic importance of a development program is that it enables a college or university to chart its growth, to anticipate emergencies, and to meet the legitimate, considered needs of all parts of the institution.

Supervised by a committee of topflight trustees and alumni, the work of the development council becomes an official part of the institution rather than a problem for the volunteer alumni group.

The development committee of the institution's board of trustees should form the nucleus of the development council.

The executive officer of the council and his job belong in the institution's uppermost scale of affairs.

Every college or university must adapt the development program to its own educational aims, its constituencies, and its available leadership.

The development program should systematically cultivate and solicit all of an institution's constituencies or "publics."

The executive officer in charge of the functioning of the development council usually gives 100 per cent of his time to it. Also, he needs an adequate staff.

Most development programs include the alumni fund.

Tax-supported colleges and universities, as well as the independent, gift-supported ones, need the "free money" which can be brought in through a well organized development program.

Colleges and universities which have the most fruitful development programs know that it costs money to get money.

REFERENCES

Chapter VI

1. Henry Adams, *The Education of Henry Adams* (Boston: Houghton Mifflin Co., 25th ed., 1924), p. 302.
2. For a helpful article on "The Development of a Development Program," see Bernard P. Taylor, *American Alumni Council News,* April 1956, pp. 6–7.
3. Council for Financial Aid to Education, *Voluntary Support of America's Colleges and Universities . . . Fiscal Year 1954–1955* (New York, 1956), p. 7.
4. James R. Reynolds, "Harvard's Search for New Money," *American Alumni Council News,* April 1956, p. 4.
5. Donald J. Cowling, "How Much Money Does a College Need?" *School and Society,* July 5, 1930, pp. 6–10.
6. Ernest Martin Hopkins, in *An Alumni Fund Survey,* Handbook Series No. 5, published by The American Alumni Council, 1932, pp. 39–40.
7. This material on Dartmouth has been drawn mainly from

George H. Colton, "Case History of Fund Raising at Dartmouth," *Report of the Thirty-eighth General Conference of The American Alumni Council, Washington, D.C., July 12–16, 1953* (Washington, D.C.: The American Alumni Council, 1953), pp. 67–72. Mr. Colton, Director of Development at Dartmouth, has supplied other data to the author.

8. C. M. O'Hearn, in a talk to members of the Yale Development Committee, November 16, 1956, at New Haven.

9. *American Alumni Council News,* March–April 1953, p. 17.

VII
The Alumni Fund

> It is, of course, largely by the extent of
> the support accorded to a college by its own
> graduates that the world judges of the right
> of that college to seek co-operation of others
> in planning for the future. An institution
> that cannot rally to its financial assistance
> the men who have taken its degrees and
> whose diploma is their passport into the
> world is in a poor position to ask assistance
> from others. It is not merely what the
> alumni give; it is the fact that they do give
> that is of supreme importance.
>
> —CHARLES W. ELIOT

The heart of a good development program is nearly always
a sound and productive annual fund, centered upon recurrent
giving by the alumni and other friends of the college. Not by
any means a new concept, this device has only in the last ten
years been exploited by a few institutions to near its full po-
tentiality. Most colleges and universities have yet to bring
their alumni funds to a point where they yield anywhere near
their maximum returns. An appreciable number, however,
have managed to reach successively higher goals in recent
years. That is as it should be; a few stirring successes touch
other institutions with the fire to achieve higher goals.

The American Alumni Council now has record of 442 colleges, universities, and schools which solicit gifts annually
from their alumni and other friends. That is not quite one-
fourth of the total number of colleges, universities, and two-
year or community colleges listed by the United States Office
of Education.

William Graham Sumner, professor of political and social science at Yale from 1872 to 1910, may have been the first man to see clearly the need for multiple and recurrent support of a college by its alumni. In 1870 he wrote:

In the first place, when we get tired of waiting for the rich man's thousands, we can begin to take the poor man's dollars. We have examples enough before us of success in business which has been won by seeing that there was more money to be made out of the pennies of the million than out of the dollars of the upper ten thousand. No graduate of the college has ever paid in full what it cost the college to educate him. A part of the expense was borne by the funds given by former benefactors of the institution. A great many can never pay the debt. A very few can, in their turn, become munificent benefactors. There is a very large number, however, between these two, who can, and would cheerfully, give according to their ability in order that the college might hold the same relative position to future generations which it held to their own. The sense of gratitude, the sense of responsibility, the enlightened interest in the cause of education, which are felt by these men, constitute a source which has never yet been tried, but which would yield richly. . . . A *popular* effort which should seize upon the indebtedness of these men to the institution and their interest in it, and make it yield money, would be a step in the right direction. If every graduate who could afford it should give the college ten dollars, and others should give more in proportion, we should enter upon a plan whose financial soundness is unquestionable. We should be paying a debt which we all owe. We should be applying principles which are thoroughly in sympathy with the ideas of this popular and democratic age, and we should reach results which we can never attain by waiting for the tardy generosity of a few men of extraordinary wealth.[1]

Sumner's concept of the idea and uses of an annual alumni fund was sound. In the light of recent developments his grasp of the importance of proportionate giving was nothing less than prescient. Indeed, his proposal as a whole was novel; it was only twenty years later, in 1890, that Yale established its alumni fund. That was the first. Dartmouth organized an annual giving program in 1906, and Wesleyan University in 1915. During the 1920's the movement gathered force, by now has become national, and is still undergoing adaptations to meet today's need for ever-increasing income.

Main Values

The chief values of the alumni fund at any college or university are four:

1. The fund ordinarily brings in unrestricted money, of which no institution of higher education ever receives enough.

2. It can generally be considered and used as a "budgeted asset" and applied to current operating expenses. To this extent it is, as many institutions call it, "living endowment."

3. The fund is not only a dependable backlog for current operations, but a feeder line. Once an alumnus or other friend forms the habit of annual giving to a college or university, it has a prospect for a capital gift now and then during his lifetime, or for a bequest.

4. A regularly contributing alumnus is a positive advocate of an institution's program, needs, and opportunities—a kind of ambassador.

The annual alumni fund has achieved its present importance because, no matter from what angle the problem of financing higher education is viewed, the regular and intelligent support of its alumni and other friends is the best capital that any college or university can have. It also encourages other financial support, especially from business corporations.

Until twenty years ago, endowment, along with income from student fees, was the most dependable financial resource of nearly every privately supported college and university. Then the abrupt changes of 1929 and afterward heightened the importance of recurrent gifts. Gradually the alumni fund became a great deal more than a mere vehicle of alumni affection. Today, in an increasing number of institutions, the annual alumni fund seeks gifts not from the alumni alone but from all possible sources: other friends, parents of students or of recent graduates, church groups, business corporations, foundations, and local organizations.

Wesleyan University several years ago took an original forward step when it created the Vanguard Fund, for which contributors are sought mainly among business men who did not have the opportunity to attend any college. Wesleyan believed rightly that non-college business leaders might desire to be associated with an American college dedicated to the training of leadership. Behind the principle of the fund is the obvious fact that the American college or university has deep roots in the nation and among its people, and logical grounds on which to ask their support of the important work that it does.

Accomplishments of Alumni Funds

The 1956 Fund Survey of The American Alumni Council showed 1,016,484 alumni giving to their respective universities, colleges, and schools. These alumni contributed a total of $36,190,198 to the 442 Funds which reported. Other alumni gifts not credited to the annual fund totaled $69,-822,733, making a grand total of $106,041,203 in alumni giving to these 442 institutions during the year.

The $36,190,198 figure in recurring annual gifts is the "living endowment" of the income at 5 per cent on $720 million, or about three times the magnificent Ford Foundation grants (1955–1956) to 630 colleges and universities for faculty salaries.

For the seventh successive year the Yale Alumni Fund, the country's oldest, received contributions from all sources in excess of $1 million. (The 1956–1957 operating cost of the Y.A.F. was 9.71 per cent of the amount raised.) Harvard

University had the largest number—34,983—of alumni contributors, and Wofford College had the largest percentage—74.4—of alumni participating. Dartmouth and Princeton followed with 70.9 and 70.7 per cent, respectively, of their alumni solicited.

Some of the figures given above are impressive. Yet a close examination of all statistics resulting from the A.A.C. survey makes it clear that the potentials of the alumni fund are far from being realized in many of the reporting institutions. Instance the fact that only 105 of the reporting 390 degree-granting United States colleges and universities had 30 per cent or more effectiveness.

For all 442 institutions reporting, the record of effectiveness was 20.5 per cent, and the average annual gift was $35.60.

Yet the extent to which the volume of annual alumni support has grown is impressive—and encouraging:

	Number of Funds Reporting	Dollar Total of Gifts
1937–38	86	$ 2,815,130
1953	302	39,786,855
1956	442	106,041,243

Improved Concepts and Techniques

A close observer of programs of annual giving to colleges and universities, Mr. Harold J. Seymour, summarized a careful review of alumni fund operations by saying: "Traditionally, the Alumni Fund has been a horizontal form of fund-raising, with little or no selectivity, with a plea rather than a case, and addressed only to alumni. It has been an annual collection, rather than a campaign." [2]

Most alumni funds appear to lack the basic essentials of effective fund-raising which have been described earlier in this book:

1. An informed and interested constituency, stimulated by facts clearly and regularly set before it.

2. A convincing and well grounded case for support.

3. A convinced and influential leadership group, lending public prestige to the college and its cause, and able to organize and lead a movement.

4. A team of co-workers thoroughly committed to the cause and both able and willing to go to the right sources and ask for money.

5. A financial program adequate to the service which the college gives to those segments of society from which it must seek support.

6. The machinery, competently manned, that is necessary to carry on fund-raising continuously as a regular administrative function of the college.

The Yale Case History

By way of demonstrating some of the potential of a well conducted alumni fund, and in addition some of the most effective techniques, it is worthwhile to examine in detail two funds which, in their respective ways, have achieved among the best results to date.

The Yale Alumni Fund, the oldest of them all, was the first to raise $1 million in a single year. This it has done seven years in a row, beginning in 1951, each time in larger amounts. In each of the last two years, 1956 and 1957, the Y.A.F. received more than $1.5 million.

It is worth stressing that the Yale Alumni Fund is an autonomous body, not a department of the university. The alumni founded it and for sixty-seven years they have run it. The founders believed at the outset that it was far better for alumni to raise money from alumni than for the university, through its officers, to go out hat in hand.

Because it has for these sixty-seven years represented an increasing flow of unrestricted money into the university's operating budget, and of reserved amounts into a separate capital fund, the alumni fund has come to have a priority status in the university's fund raising. If the university or any of its schools is obliged to seek capital gifts, this search is accommodated to the uninterrupted functioning of the alumni fund. "The one remains; the many change and pass."

Yale has learned that the alumni fund is a means by which its graduates can give according to their means, and without pressure and gladly. The university has come to believe that such giving under low pressure is best, and knows from experience that it plants in the alumni a realization of the university's continuing needs. Regular giving like this can, and often does, lead to substantial giving outside of the alumni fund.

John W. Sterling, of the class of 1864, was a Rockefeller lawyer. A bachelor, he worked hard, prospered, and regularly gave his mite to the alumni fund. Yale was hardly aware of his growing financial ability, and during his lifetime had no hint of his design: to save money and to leave it to Yale. Under his will his bequest to the university amounted to approximately $15 million, and by the time the university came into possession of it the value had increased to approximately $30 million.

Yale has received few single benefactions of that magnitude, but in all, through the alumni fund, it has been given nearly $30 million in the period 1890–1957.

Naturally, the management of the fund for two-thirds of a century has built a solid core of experience. From it certain principles can be drawn by any college or university fund—in spite of the fact that every institution has of course to build its organization according to conditions which are peculiar to it. Here at any rate are some instructive facts about the Yale Alumni Fund.

ORGANIZATION

The board of directors is composed of thirty-five alumni, seven of them elected in each year and all of them for five-year terms. There are also eight ex-officio members: the managing director of the alumni fund, its secretary, and its treasurer; the chairman of the alumni board, and its executive secretary; the president of the association of class secretaries; the executive director of the office of university development; and the assistant to the president of the university.

The officers of the fund are the chairman, the vice chairman, the managing director, the secretary, the treasurer, the university director, and four assistant chairmen, each of whom is responsible for a specific part of the fund's operations. These officers are elected by the board of directors for a two-year period. Normally the board meets twice a year in New York, in January and in June.

On the other hand, the ten officers of the fund, who compose the executive committee of the board of directors, meet from time to time as a policy-making group. In November and December they convene almost weekly, and monthly thereafter until the campaign ends on June 30.

In brief, the organization of the Yale Alumni Fund provides for a regular rotation in its board which insures a flow of fresh talent and energy. And both are needed, for the board of directors is a hard-working group. Yale appears to have been more than ordinarily fortunate in the quality of leadership that the directors have given to the fund; that is probably half the secret of its success.

SECRETARIAT

Working with the "pilot house," which is in New York, is an "engine room crew" of twenty located in New Haven. The managing director, the secretary, and two assistant secretaries head the staff. The secretary works with the class agents, and the assistant secretaries are in charge of the regional effort and the bequest program.

The Yale Alumni Fund is a vast operation, and it requires adequate staffing and a good deal of specialization, as a look at the personnel chart suggests: office manager and assistant, three secretaries, three bookkeepers, two addressograph operators, and five direct mail or clerical workers. The staff not only does the fundamental work of the annual campaign but, during the year, keeps accurate files, acknowledges gifts (very necessary), compiles statistics and reports, and publishes literature and the annual report, an important document which for years the Yale Alumni Fund has prepared well.

CLASS AGENT ORGANIZATION

Class agents, varying in number from class to class, are appointed with the approval of the fund officers. Some of the older classes each have one agent, many classes have between two and five, and all of the classes since 1935, when the residential college plan was put into operation, have one agent for each of the ten colleges.

Agents for each graduating class are selected in the spring before commencement. On their behalf two or three instructional meetings are held in the fund office, and every fall a convocation of fund workers is held in New Haven over a football weekend. Meetings in the form of discussion groups are held Friday afternoon, Friday evening, and Saturday morning. The working sessions at these convocations are divided in five ways: reunion agents, non-reunion agents, regional chairmen, bequest chairmen, and agents for classes from 1935 to the present. In addition, a dinner meeting is held in New York once a year which is addressed by the chairman of the fund and the president of the university.

Presidents of the Yale Associations throughout the country select the regional chairmen, with the approval of the officers of the fund.

These directors know the importance of recognition for achievement; hence awards are given each year to class agents and regional chairmen, in the form of scrolls signed by the president of the university. Moreover, recognition for various accomplishments is given from time to time in the *Yale Alumni Magazine,* as well as in the alumni fund annual report. All fund workers are also given priority on applications for seats at football games played in the Yale Bowl.

REGIONAL PROGRAM

Yale now has regional committees organized in 190 localities situated in 34 states, the District of Columbia, Hawaii, Cuba, Venezuela, and Peru. In the fourth month of the alumni fund's five-month campaign, these committees approach only those alumni who have not contributed thus far in the campaign. Because of distance and geographical barriers, the class agents can reach only a small percentage of their respective classes. Regional committee members are able to approach Yale alumni personally at the local level.

Primarily, they are supposed to increase the number of contributors rather than the size of gifts. Records show how efficacious the regional committee work is. About 70 per cent of Yale's alumni live in areas that are covered by the regional solicitation. In 1957, 62 per cent of the alumni living in these regional areas contributed, as against 51 per cent where no regional committees were operative.

SCHEDULE

In the light of long experience, the timing and approach of the whole alumni fund campaign have been worked out with infinite pains. The first mailing date is December 1, when a letter with a reminder of tax advantages is sent to all alumni who contributed more than $50 in the previous campaign. This is an auto-typed letter signed by the chairman of the fund. Class agents' letters are mailed on February 1, March 15, and May 1. Only alumni who have not already contributed receive the second two letters. On June 1 the chairman sends a letter of reminder to all alumni who have not given by that time.

The class agents have their choice of posting their own letters or having them sent from the fund office. If they elect the second course, they are urged at least to sign their letters and add personal postscripts. Interestingly, most of the older agents like to prepare and post their own letters.

A matter of fundamental importance is selectivity. In recent years, during which the fund total has passed the $1 million mark seven times in a row, the fund has strongly recommended that the 10 per cent who have been "screened" as having the highest giving potential be approached first by the class agents, by a personal call or by telephone or by a direct personal letter. This feature is the "special gifts" technique taken over from the typical campaign for capital gifts. It pays, for normally the Yale Alumni Fund receives 73 per cent of the annual total from less than 11 per cent of the number of contributors. Many classes have special gifts chairmen, who may or may not use committees in their work.

GRADUATE AND PROFESSIONAL SCHOOLS

Naturally, since many of the Yale graduate and professional schools alumni did not attend Yale as undergraduates, their primary loyalty remains with the colleges from which they received their baccalaureate degrees. Beginning in 1949, however, the Yale Alumni Fund adopted a plan under which money contributed by alumni of all professional schools is turned over to the deans to be used in their discretion, after a pro rata share of the expenses has been deducted. The result has been a steady growth in numbers of contributors and in amounts contributed. For example, in 1954–1955 a total of 5,213 graduate and professional school alumni contributed $79,899 to the Y.A.F.; in 1956–1957, the number of contributors rose to 6,852, and the total of gifts to $98,303.

The law, medical, art, and drama Schools use the Yale College system of class agents. Alumni of the graduate and other professional schools receive letters of appeal from agents regardless of class. Graduate school alumni receive letters of request from the dean.

It is by now evident that graduate and professional school alumni are willing to contribute to the Yale Alumni Fund if their gifts are applied to the graduate schools which they attended.

SOLICITATION OF PARENTS

As a background for parental solicitation, Yale on a Saturday each autumn has a Parents Day to which the university invites all parents of undergraduate students. The president welcomes the parents and one of the masters of the residential colleges addresses them. Afterward they have luncheon with their sons in their respective residential colleges, and then attend a football game. After the game, the masters hold receptions in all of the residential colleges, and the freshman dean holds a reception in Commons for the parents of freshmen.

The parents committee itself, made up generally of twenty-five to thirty members, is appointed each year by the fund office after consultation with university officials, especially the director of the enrollment and scholarship committee. During the campaign three letters are mailed, all signed by the chairman of the parents committee, and that is the only solicitation directed to the fathers and mothers of recent students in Yale College.

The contribution of the parents committee is this:

Year	Number of Gifts	Amount
1950–51	263	$21,418
1951–52	761	37,252
1954–55	947	38,461
1955–56	1,002	44,318
1956–57	1,034	46,800

In 1956–1957 the Yale Alumni Fund solicited, in addition to the parents of students enrolled in all four of the undergraduate classes, those of the classes of 1950 through 1956.

REUNION CLASS SPECIAL FUNDS

These, in the total scale of the Yale Alumni Fund, are of great importance, as a glance at the accompanying table will indicate. Approximately 20 per cent of all Yale classes hold reunions each year, starting in the fifth year after graduation. It has been traditional since the fund was started for these reunion classes to contribute a larger amount than in non-reunion years. In the last few years, reunion gifts have approximated three to five times the amounts given in non-reunion years.

Formerly it was the custom to put all reunion-class gifts into the principal of the fund. Whether or not to do so is now subject to the vote of the board of directors. In recent years most, if not all, of the money raised has been given to the university for current operating expenses. The principal of the fund now stands at the impressive total of $5,427,341.

The record of the last five twenty-fifth reunion class gifts is as follows:

Class	Number of Living Contributors	Amount
1928 "Ac" and "Sheff" combined *	587	$113,980
1929 "Ac" and "Sheff" combined	555	135,823
1930 "Ac" and "Sheff" combined	538	120,000
1931 "Ac" and "Sheff" combined	660	210,000
1932 "Ac" and "Sheff" combined	515	133,014

Yale, like Princeton, now has a gift insurance program. Starting with the class of 1948, every member of each class is asked to take out a twenty-five-year endowment policy. The

* In 1945 the Sheffield Scientific School ceased to be an undergraduate department of the university and became, according to the original intention of the donor of the endowment, Yale's graduate department in the fields of science. "Ac" refers to Yale College.

money received at the end of twenty-five years is to be used as the twenty-fifth reunion gift of the class to the alumni fund. During senior year ten classes have now set up such programs, and virtually all of the ten have reached the $250,000 face-value goal on the aggregate of these insurance policies. The aggregate of the ten class programs is now $2,497,629.

The theory works in practice: it is better to spread reunion class contributions over twenty-five years than to try to get such large sums from a single class in one year. Policies taken out by members of Yale's most recent ten graduating classes average about $11 a year a man. Approximately 80 per cent of each class has taken the policies.

ALUMNI FUND AND THE BEQUEST PROGRAM

Committees have been appointed from time to time to prepare the ground for a full-scale bequest program, but none came into being until 1953. Each year, however, a statement about bequests is contained in the alumni fund annual report, as well as a standard form of bequest. This form also appears in various catalogues of the university.

In 1953–1954 the Yale Alumni Fund organized a bequest program along well tested lines. A letter is sent each year to each member of classes which are holding twenty-fifth, thirtieth, thirty-fifth, fortieth, forty-fifth, and fiftieth reunions, with the suggestion that those men who wish to do so can perpetuate their annual gifts, after death, by making bequests to the alumni fund. By 1958–1959 this plan will be in effect in all classes that have held a twenty-fifth reunion. It is expected that a member of each class, probably not a class agent, will be appointed the bequest chairman of that class.

RELATIONSHIP OF THE ALUMNI FUND TO THE UNIVERSIT'
DEVELOPMENT PROGRAM

Because of its record as a producer of both income and of capital, the Yale Alumni Fund has been given top priority in fund-raising by the corporation of the university. No alumnus is asked to contribute to any desired capital fund at the risk of his reducing his usual gift to the alumni fund. In practice, the alumni fund and the office of university development work together very closely. If a capital-gifts program is contemplated by any school of the university, such as forestry and engineering in different years recently, the managing director of the alumni fund and the director of the office of university development have to be consulted before permission is granted.

RECORD OF THE YALE ALUMNI FUND

The total contributed to the fund in the period 1890–1957 is approaching $30 million. The brief record given here makes it clear that the real potential of the alumni fund is only now beginning to be realized.

Year	Number of Contributors	Total in Gifts
1890	385	$ 11,015
		(plus $5,000 in pledges)
1944	15,203	292,946
1945	15,511	331,034
1947	15,846	401,753
1949	18,725	508,765
1950	21,230	770,182
1951	24,698	1,010,324
1952	24,242	1,015,418
1953	24,854	1,021,832
1954	25,607	1,083,123
1955	26,555	1,260,779
1956	27,969	1,514,068
1957	30,500	1,736,837

The total of the principal of the fund is at present $5,427,-341. In 1957, after operating expenses of $159,340 were deducted and $98,303 was given to the graduate and professional schools, the sum of $1,479,194 was turned over to the university for current expenses, in addition to $217,533 in interest on the principal of the fund. The total "gift" to the university from the alumni fund was thus $1,671,031 for the year 1957. To the principal of the alumni fund a total of $46,185 was added during the year.

PERCENTAGE COST

During recent years the costs of operation have been close to 10 per cent of the amount raised. In 1956–1957 the cost was 9.71 per cent, a reasonable figure.

PROPORTIONATE GIVING

This, it will be recalled, was in Professor Sumner's mind in 1870. Only now are a number of colleges and universities, mainly in the so-called "Ivy League," translating this phrase into a broader pattern of giving.

Yale in particular has calculated with care the effect of proportionate giving, and considers that the $1.5 million-plus total reached annually in 1956 and 1957 is merely a floor and not a ceiling. The university has record of approximately 40,-000 men living who attended Yale as undergraduates. By test it believes that not more than 10 per cent of these 40,000 are unable to give, and that not more than another 10 per cent are uninterested in Yale.

What is the potential giving power of the remaining 80 per cent? The university calculates that if all of them gave as one quarter of them now give, Yale would receive $2.25 million each year through the alumni fund. If each of them gave, over his lifetime, an amount equal to the subsidy which the university provided for him during his attendance (it costs the university $1,268 a year more for each student than the student pays), together with interest, Yale would receive at least $3.7 million each year.

Another study in upgrading, which the Yale Alumni Fund developed for use in its 1956–1957 campaign, might also have wider applicability. The essence of it follows:

Dollar Range	Number of Contributors	Average Gift	Increase in amount if each person in group increased to the minimum of the next group
$ 0–9.99	8,479	$ 4.73	$ 44,630.83
10–24.99	11,643	12.91	140,682.98
25–49.99	5,005	28.13	109,421.75
50–99.99	2,283	56.51	99,279.00
100–199.99	1,848	113.15	160,489.85
200–499.99	720	267.38	167,485.14
500 and over	637	1,328.03	—
		Total Increase	$721,989.55

Upgrading in the brackets below $50 would alone yield more than $300,000 additional a year.

In a booklet entitled "A Challenge for Yale and You" which the Yale Alumni Fund issued in 1953, a check sheet was provided as a means of assisting individual alumni and business corporations to determine their proportionate giving to 1) religion, 2) education, 3) community services, and 4) world services. It was suggested that anyone with a balanced interest in all four areas could start with an arbitrary yard-stick of 30–30–30 and 10 per cent for areas 1, 2, 3, and 4 respectively, modifying these proportions according to individual loyalties and interests.

What, when the scales are all balanced, is the incentive for contributing to Yale (or any college or university)? The Yale Alumni Fund has always been careful to base its appeal on facts. This special booklet pointed out that to Yale, since 1945, the fund has become a deciding factor as to whether the university goes forward or backward. The fund is represented, rightly, as sustaining a program of progress for all aspects of the university's work; and, conversely, is preventing otherwise certain deterioration. In the booklet, the four areas in which gifts to the Yale Alumni Fund help the university are shown as: 1) scholarship aid, 2) faculty salaries, 3) running the plant, and 4) additional facilities.

And this factual appeal is ended, skillfully, on an emotional note: "So that our sons may have the same advantages, send your contributions today."

The Dartmouth Alumni Fund

The Dartmouth Alumni Council also conducts an annual campaign, through a five-man alumni fund committee. In type of organization and in size of headquarters personnel, the Dartmouth Alumni Fund and the Yale Alumni Fund bear a close resemblance. But there are differences in detail and in method of operation, and in some areas Dartmouth has worked out techniques of exceptional value.

Perhaps more than any other major educational institution in the East, Dartmouth has emphasized the "living endowment" concept—alumni contributing each year the equivalent of income from endowment, an annual campaign year after year rather than occasional capital-gifts "drives" for endowment. The purpose of the alumni fund consistently has been to provide the marginal current funds which enable Dartmouth to give service each year beyond what the limits of its endowment and tuition fees permit. The importance of the fund to Dartmouth was illustrated in 1957, for example, when the Dartmouth Alumni Fund produced the equivalent of the income on $25 million, more than half the total endowment of the college; and when receipts from the fund were actually used to meet 12 per cent of the college's expenses.

CLASS AGENT ORGANIZATION

The fund has sixty-seven head class agents and provides team assistance for them through 1,500 class agents and newsletter editors. In all of the larger classes, the head agent requires the help of a number of classmates; so the class agent has the all-important job of approaching personally an assigned group of classmates. As underlined in the Dartmouth Alumni Fund's excellent "Campaign Handbook," his objective is to get a gift from each man assigned to him, "a realistic gift, proportionate to the individual's giving ability."

Dartmouth believes thoroughly in the well tested campaign principle that personal solicitation is the most effective means of procuring a gift.

ORDER OF SOLICITATION

Dartmouth also begins its annual campaign with a "special gifts" solicitation. Based on selectivity, this advance campaign is started in December, when an advance gift mailing (auto-typed letters) is sent to all men who gave $100 or more in the previous year. Four general mailings are sent from Dartmouth Alumni Fund headquarters about April 1, May 1, June 1, and June 15. But from April 1 to June 30, when it ends, the campaign is in the hands of the class agent organization, and each class runs its own campaign in its own way. This fact prevents campaign procedures and techniques from becoming stereotyped.

PARENTS' COMMITTEE

A separate committee of fifty persons was organized in 1951 with a non-Dartmouth parent as chairman. This committee operates largely through direct mail solicitation, which has proved to be fairly effective. In 1957 the fund received 1,368 parents' gifts totaling $57,000. Included in the mailing list are all non-Dartmouth parents of students, and parents represented in classes two years out of college as well as in selected classes farther back.

CLASS MEMORIAL FUNDS

These are sought by twenty-fifth reunion classes. In 1938, the class of 1913 started the custom of making a capital gift to the college beyond its gifts to the alumni fund, and each

succeeding class has done so. These capital gifts after nine-
teen years total over $1.5 million, and are known as class
memorial funds. Interest from them is added to the alumni
fund each year.

Seven out of ten of the most recent twenty-fifth reunion
classes have exceeded $100,000 goals. Solicitation for the
alumni fund is combined with solicitation for the capital fund
in the twenty-fifth year.

In 1951 Dartmouth organized a bequest program with a
bequest chairman in each class, and already is finding a close
causal relationship between giving to the alumni fund and the
making of bequests to Dartmouth.

RECORD OF THE ALUMNI FUND

Like nearly all others, the Dartmouth Alumni Fund had a
modest beginning, but has built up an enormously effective
organization which in 1957 procured gifts from 71.3 per cent
of the graduates and non-graduates of the College. The results
achieved down the years are interesting:

Year	Number of Contributors	Total in Gifts
1915	536	$ 6,580
1944	13,509	284,565
1951	15,417	577,263
1952	16,146	611,531
1954	18,259	700,365
1956	20,107	864,230
1957	20,714	928,592

USE OF THE ALUMNI FUND

The trustees of Dartmouth College, meeting in October,
set the budget for the academic year. They estimate the college's needs according to their own information and standards,
and then request the alumni fund to furnish so much revenue
for the year's budget. This sum, to repeat, is considered by the

college as a "budgeted asset." In recent years an important aspect of the alumni fund campaign to raise this sum has been that any surplus is placed in the college's scholarship program.

Beyond that, the Dartmouth Alumni Fund has no principal, such as the Yale Alumni Fund has accumulated.

Development of Techniques of Special Value by Princeton

Princeton's annual giving, started in 1940, has grown rapidly both in the techniques developed and in the results achieved. Princeton was among the first universities to develop regional committees on a national scale. And, almost more than any other, the Princeton University Fund has devoted itself to backing up faculty salaries.

The fund officers emphasize that personal calls are the keystone of regional committee work. Solicitation by mail is the function of the class agents, who are important in fund activities.

But in these days of multiple appeals for many causes there is nothing as effective as a visit *in person*. Most men are too busy to read, but there is scarcely a man who will not listen to a fellow alumnus who takes the trouble to come and see him. Despite all that has been printed on the subject, there are still thousands of alumni who do not grasp the vital importance to American Education, and to Princeton in particular, of their thoughtful support.[3]

The regional organization and the class agents do not compete, but work together. However, the Princeton system of regional committees differs from that of Dartmouth, for instance, in one major respect. A regional chairman in the Princeton University Fund is supreme within his area and covers all the men in it, irrespective of class. But the regional chairman reports to the university fund office. In the seven chief Princeton alumni centers (Baltimore, Chicago, New York, Philadelphia, Pittsburgh, Princeton, and Washington) where organization tends to follow class lines, Princeton comes closer to Dartmouth's reliance on the class agents. These may be enlisted by Princeton's regional chairmen because of the number of men involved, but in every area the regional chairman is still in charge.[4]

The executive director of the Princeton University Fund warns that a regional organization is in effect a national sales organization with branch offices, and will require service. He advises: "To those who are starting such an effort, I would earnestly recommend that you begin on a trial basis with the most likely towns on your list. This will give you experience in the requirements. . . . Above all else, keep your areas reasonable." [5]

Princeton also has been notably successful in developing techniques to increase the size of contributions. In "Signal Practice," the 1957 handbook, the advice is:

Ask directly for larger contributions than last year. This is *not* a difficult or embarrassing thing to do. It is merely a matter of phrasing—*but the phrasing is important.*

If a man who gave $10 last year is asked to consider giving $25 this year and asks why the solicitor thinks he can, the answer might be:

I don't *think* you can—I'm asking you to *consider* doing it. And the reason I put it that way is simply this—I've asked other men the same question and it amazes me how many say "Why sure, Fred, I could give you $25—didn't realize you wanted contributions like that—I've been sending in $10 every year, out of habit I guess—in fact, I guess I never thought much about it one way or the other.

That, in a nutshell, is what has been our trouble—the thousands of men who give "the same as last year," out of sheer habit, and who *never think much about it one way or the other,* meaning whether they could increase their contributions. You will indeed be amazed at the results of giving a man a specific amount to think about (you are not *asking* for it).[6]

Again, Princeton has found that most men periodically have a better than normal year. They could increase their regular contributions, but do not want to be "tabbed" at a higher figure than they think they may be able to maintain. The Princeton University Fund has the answer: let each man make the larger gift and stipulate that X dollars of it be recorded as "extra this year." It is so recorded by the class agent and the fund. During 1956 a total of 1,161 Princeton alumni sent in such "extras."

Lastly, the Princeton University Fund has made the improvement of faculty salaries and status its first concern. The fund set a goal of $2 million for its 1957 annual giving campaign, as another step to realize substantial faculty salary increases. Princeton in effect asked alumni, parents of students, and other friends to give double the amount that was asked in 1955, and $500,000 more than the 1956 figure.

In launching the 1957 annual giving, George J. Cooke, Jr., executive director of the Princeton University Fund, pointed out that a full professor at Princeton currently receives an income which gives him 77.5 per cent of the purchasing power he had in 1940. (In contrast, in 1954 the purchasing power of factory workers was 143 per cent of its 1940 value.) To restore the 1940 purchasing power of Princeton's faculty would require an additional $800,000 a year.[7]

The Wofford College Story

Colleges whose constituencies may be assumed to have a lesser giving potential than the alumni of Dartmouth, Princeton, and Yale probably would demur that each of these institutions is unique. This is in a measure true. The fact remains, however, that the alumni council in each of these institutions has realized its need for steady annual dollar aid, and has accepted a responsibility for supplying it. Moreover, these groups have recognized that theirs is the prime responsibility for furnishing aid sufficient to enable the institution to continue to do a quality job. "God helps those who help themselves"—in institutional fund-raising as in other fields. A college or university whose alumni are not supporting it financially stands on a weak leg when it applies elsewhere for assistance.

As a matter of fact, the principles on which the alumni funds of Dartmouth, Princeton, and Yale conduct their annual giving campaigns have wide applicability.

Consider Wofford College, a small liberal arts college for men (750) connected with the Methodist Church and located at Spartanburg, South Carolina. In September 1955, President Pendleton Gaines received a letter from his friend Roger Milliken, Wofford trustee and president of the Deering-Milliken Company (textiles). A Yale graduate, Mr. Milliken wrote: "The New England colleges . . . have been notably successful in raising funds through an annual program of giving. . . . It seems to me that this is a splendid untapped source of potential support for Wofford."

To stimulate development of a similar program at Wofford, Mr. Milliken agreed to underwrite the expense of ascertaining how Dartmouth, Princeton, and Yale organized their annual giving programs. He agreed further to contribute to Wofford $1,000 for each percentage point of increase in the 1956 annual giving over the 1955 result of 12 per cent.

Wofford's alumni director visited Hanover, Princeton, and New Haven for briefing by the three alumni fund directors. Then the pace quickened at Spartanburg. Wofford's alumni president appointed a central alumni fund committee to take charge of the intensive campaign he knew was a prelude to success. During October and November this committee laid out a concentrated program of letter writing and personal solicitation. In mid-December a letter signed by the committee chairman was sent to the 6,000 living alumni for whom Wofford had addresses.

A steady flow of letters containing contributions and pledges began at once to arrive. Class agents returned to the campus for a workshop at which they planned a series of personal letters. The first class agent mailing raised the contributions of the alumni to 15 per cent—a new record for the college. At this point Mr. Milliken made his first payment, $3,000, to President Gaines.

Newsletters went out every two weeks to area presidents, fund chairmen, and class agents. Competition among them was fired up.

But it was clear that personal solicitation also was necessary. In each alumni association area a fund committee was organized, with a general chairman and county chairman as needed. Personal solicitation was launched. More class agent letters were posted, plus a general letter to all alumni telling them of the forthcoming "Fund Facts" bulletin, which would list all donors to date. This was mailed three weeks later.

By late spring 1956, the percentage of alumni donors had reached 41 per cent, and soon thereafter 59 per cent.

By November it became evident that Wofford, under a still greater head of steam, could set a national record for alumni participation in the annual giving. Television program time in Charlotte and Spartanburg was contributed to Wofford, and programs were prepared for early November.

At about this time a letter with a string attached was sent to all non-donors. Each was asked to tie the string around a finger so that he would remember to send his contribution before Mr. Milliken's offer expired on November 30. This device was successful.

By mid-November, as a result of the letter and the television programs, a mark of 63.6 per cent alumni participation had been reached. Then came the great push. Three newsletter memoranda were sent during the last two weeks of November to campaign workers, stating simply: "Only __ days left! The percentage is now _____. We need _____ contributors."

Late in November a "day letter" was telegraphed to each area president, fund chairman, and class agent urging him to communicate with every non-responding alumnus in his county.

During the last few days of November, Wofford received as many as 100 to 150 contributions a day. And in this period college administrative officers, when possible, put aside their regular duties and personally called on non-contributors whose names they had selected from a list. The alumni director reported: "No part of the drive was more successful or inspiring than this. These officials brought in a contribution from nearly every alumnus on their lists."

When the counters were all in, 74.4 per cent of the Wofford alumni who were solicited were found to have contributed—4,276 donors out of 5,750 alumni with known addresses. The percentage for graduates was 79.9 per cent.

Wofford's 74.4 per cent effectiveness record for 1956 enabled it to surpass Dartmouth and Princeton (70.9 per cent and 70.7 per cent respectively), which for years had led all annual giving in this respect.

During the 1956 alumni fund campaign Wofford alumni contributed $53,773 to the college, an average of $12.58 each. Mr. Milliken was delighted to give Wofford more than $62,000, in accordance with his agreement. And he underscored the main fact of the year's achievement: that Wofford alumni had learned they must help their college before they can expect others to do so. During 1955 the college's annual giving deferred to its 100th Anniversary Development Program, which netted $379,755. In 1956, annual giving alone brought in $115,773.

Wofford attributes its success to four major factors: 1) the incentive of Mr. Milliken's challenge, 2) well organized area associations and well planned solicitation procedures, 3) an alumni office alert to the plans and mechanics of the campaign, and 4) the conscientious efforts of the area workers in personal solicitation.[8]

Wofford has furnished the answer complete to skeptics or shirkers who protest that what has worked for others will not necessarily work for them because "our school" does not have a long history of devoted alumni interest and support. Loren L. Hickerson, of the State University of Iowa, a former president of the American Alumni Council, calls this the "weakest kind of rationalization," and contends: " 'Our school' never will have that kind of history unless we set out to build it, in our own places and at our own levels, through the only investments which will do this or any other great job—brains and money." [9]

What Mr. Hickerson is talking about and what Wofford achieved, it is important to realize, is rooted in the student experience of the alumni—what happened to them in their four undergraduate years on the campus. Clarence A. Schoenfeld, of the University of Wisconsin, has put the matter succinctly:

It is really too late, of course, to woo an individual if you wait until he is an alumnus. The time and place to develop alumni loyalty is during the undergraduate years and on the campus. The student who has had good teachers, is given wise counsel and helpful individual attention, and is oriented to a sense of obligation and responsibility during his college career is generally the student who becomes a staunch old grad.[10]

The Wofford achievement, as it relates to the experience of "wealthy schools" like Dartmouth, Harvard, Princeton, and Yale, directs attention to another fact: in the 1956 Alumni Fund Report of the American Alumni Council, thirty-one funds reported gifts higher in the average than those made to the four "Ivy League" institutions mentioned. Manifestly, some of these thirty-one funds were conducting capital-gifts campaigns through the alumni organization during the year;

a few indeed specified the fulfilment of building needs as among the purposes of the alumni fund for 1956. On the other hand, twenty-five of these thirty-one—like Dartmouth, Princeton, and Yale—sought and employed the year's contributions from the alumni for the general or unrestricted (among other) uses of the colleges concerned.

Clearly, however, in spite of the marked advances in the last ten years, most of the 442 alumni funds reporting in 1956 to the American Alumni Council have their ripest achievements still ahead of them. Fundamental techniques of annual campaigning which in a limited number of colleges and universities have brought such excellent results are worth close study and adaptation. Many alumni councils have yet to draw fully upon proven methods and experiences in the endeavor to help their institutions further. It is worth their consideration that most corporations—now hopefully regarded as the one great untapped source of support for higher education in this country—although they feel they have both a responsibility and an opportunity as "corporate citizens," are much interested to know to what extent the various colleges are being helped by their own alumni.

Annual Giving and Capital-Gifts Campaigns

Lastly, what about annual giving and capital-gifts campaigns?

As explained in Chapter V, capital-gifts campaigns have their useful place among the fund-raising techniques which colleges and universities may employ. However, such campaigns generally have the best chance of success when the alumni and other constituencies are habituated to annual giving. In fund-raising, this is a college's main power plant. Other engines are auxiliary.

Most experienced heads believe that in the event an intensive campaign for capital funds has to be made, it should be fitted in with but should not displace the annual giving. Two major universities which in the last decade have made special gifts appeals suspended the annual giving during the intensive campaign. After they resumed the annual giving, several years of costly effort were required to regain its effectiveness. This is the general experience of colleges and universities everywhere.

Moreover, in most capital-gifts campaigns, 10 to 15 per cent of the contributors usually give 75 per cent or more of the dollar total. Logic appears to be on the side of selection, rather than mass appeal, in the search for capital funds. Annual giving seems best suited to the financial ability of most alumni of most colleges and universities.

President Emeritus Seymour of Yale used to like to tell a story illustrating the point. Two dowagers visited a silver fox farm and were given a guided tour by the owner. Near the end of it one of the ladies asked him how many pelts he was able to get from each silver fox. He replied, "Lady, we find that if you skin them more than once a year, they get very, very nervous." [11] So with alumni.

Summary

The heart of a good development program is nearly always a sound and productive annual giving.

Most colleges and universities have yet to bring their alumni funds to a point where they yield anywhere near their maximum returns. Less than one-fourth of the nation's institutions of higher education are known to solicit gifts annually from their alumni and other friends.

The main values of the annual giving are that a) it ordinarily brings in unrestricted money, b) it can generally be used as a "budgeted asset" and applied to current operating expenses, c) it is not only a dependable backlog for current operations, but a feeder line for occasional capital gifts or bequests, and d) a regularly contributing alumnus or other friend is a kind of ambassador for the institution.

The regular and intelligent support of its alumni and other friends is the best capital that any college or university can have.

The most successful annual giving programs are conducted as *annual campaigns* rather than *collections,* and use some of the basic techniques of capital-gifts appeals: hard facts and a sound case, strong leadership and an enthusiastic volunteer corps working toward stated goals, personal solicitation, sound organization (including regional), and selectivity, among others. Class agents and regional chairmen are almost indispensable to a strong annual giving program.

In charge of special personnel, a bequest program can be conducted simultaneously with the annual giving.

Various methods of upgrading gifts, to insure proportionate giving and to surmount token contributions, have been devised and may be used profitably.

It is necessary to spend money in order to raise money.

Extra gifts in "good years" may be expected from a certain number of alumni.

With energy and intelligence, any college or university can develop an effective annual giving program.

When capital-gifts campaigns are necessary, they should be fitted in with, but should not displace, even temporarily, the annual giving.

REFERENCES

Chapter VII

1. Harris E. Starr, *William Graham Sumner* (New York: Henry Holt and Company, 1925), pp. 87–88.
2. Harold J. Seymour, private memorandum, December 1950, "Notes on Annual Giving to Colleges and Universities," p. 4.
3. Princeton University 1957 handbook, "Signal Practice," p. 12.

4. George J. Cooke, Jr., *American Alumni Council News,* January 1954, p. 19, *passim.*
5. *Ibid.*
6. "Signal Practice," pp. 8–9.
7. *The New York Times,* November 2, 1957, p. 66.
8. For a fuller story on Wofford, see T. Keller Cogswell, "A Challenge Pays off in Percentages," *American Alumni Council News,* April 1957, pp. 12–13.
9. Quoted in Ernest T. Stewart, Jr., "Alumni Support and Annual Giving," reprinted from *The Annals of the American Academy of Political and Social Science,* September 1955, p. 129.
10. Clarence A. Schoenfeld, *The University and Its Publics* (New York: Harper & Brothers, 1954), p. 221.
11. Ernest T. Stewart, *op. cit.,* p. 126.

VIII *Other Constituencies*

> He showed me his bill of fare to tempt me
> to dine with him; poh, said I, I value not
> your bill of fare, give me your bill of
> company.
>
> —SWIFT, *Journal to Stella*

James E. Armstrong, Alumni Secretary of the University of Notre Dame, has said about the defining of sources of financial support for American higher education: "College presidents wrote *all* the chapters of the old testament of fund raising in the first 250 years of financing higher education in this country. Then Yale discovered the alumni." [1]

Institutions the country over are still discovering their multiple constituencies, starting with their alumni. Moreover, most of the colleges and universities which have identified these "publics" are still learning how to cultivate them effectively.

In the survey of voluntary support in the fiscal year 1954–1955, conducted by the Council for Financial Aid to Education in co-operation with the American College Public Relations Association, these main sources of contributions were identified:

1. Alumni.
2. Other individuals and/or families.
3. Non-alumni, non-church groups.
4. Business corporations.
5. General welfare foundations.
6. Governing board of institution.
7. Governments.

8. Religious denominations.
9. Bequests.
10. Trusts, annuities, and life contracts.

Sources 4, 5, 9, and 10—and how to approach them—are described in later chapters of this book. Here it is timely to consider parents (under 2), friends and associates (under 3), religious denominations, and the Federal Government.

In working with these groups, colleges and universities have to proceed, as in all other areas, on the basic principle that understanding precedes giving. Here an inexorable pull takes us back to the two-way street: colleges and universities which ask for personal interest and financial support must be prepared to give something—and they have great gifts to offer. In each instance, the manner of cultivation is of fundamental importance.

Parents

CARLETON COLLEGE

No college or university has succeeded better than Carleton College in cultivating the parents of its students and winning their interest and support.

When it established its alumni fund in 1942, Carleton counted the parents of students as members of the Carleton community. In 1943, Carleton started careful cultivation of the parents. It selected non-alumni parents whose children were not receiving financial aid—parents of students currently enrolled and parents whose children had been students within the previous five years, whether they had been graduated or not.

Carleton organized a number of parents' committees in different states. These committees were merely sponsors. It was not until several years later that any of them were asked to make calls or do any other special work. By 1957 the college had consolidated these various committees into two: one for

Illinois, from which about 25 per cent of Carleton's students come, and one for the remainder of the country.

In some years the Carleton College Alumni Fund sends the same mailing piece to alumni and to parents. At other times the fund addresses each group separately. When the alumni fund has area meetings, parents are invited as members of the Carleton community.

Annually the alumni fund staff goes through the parents' files and removes the names of people who have shown no sign of interest within a five-year period.

Since its parents' program was started, Carleton has added a Parents' Day, which merely furnishes "background music" for the general program. Parents' Day at Northfield is held in October and is built around a convocation addressed by the president. Also there are a luncheon, usually a football game, and then a tea attended by faculty members, too. The attendance taxes the college's facilities.

Contributions from parents are counted in Carleton's annual alumni fund totals, regardless of the purposes for which they are intended. Alumni contributions are counted in the same way, and the two groups of gifts are combined to reach the year's over-all total.

In the three years 1954, 1955, and 1956 Carleton received annually an average of $213,000 in gifts from the parents of students or former students.[2]

WILLIAMS COLLEGE

Williams College began cultivating the parents of its students only in 1954, twelve years later than Carleton, but did so in ways that should be enlightening to other colleges and universities. Before putting its parents' program into action, Williams had the method of cultivation under close study for a year or two. An alumnus and former trustee was in charge of the study. He knew merchandising, and applied to the project at Williams the business philosophy that if you want to get money you have to give goods or services.

Here are the services on which the parents' program at Williams are based:

1. Before the student enters college provide him with materials about Williams: handbooks, leaflets, etc. This device will make the boy feel wanted and at home, and will give his parents the feeling that "these people think of everything."

2. Send the parents notice of their boy's student and faculty advisers. This gesture provides another useful contact with the parents, and lets them know that the college is interested in their boy.

3. Encourage the house president, if the boy joins a fraternity, to write his parents, telling them about his forthcoming membership, as well as something about the history of the organization, its purposes, and its costs.

4. Entertain the parents when they first visit the campus, after the beginning of term, and show them the institution. At Williams, the president and his wife hold a tea and reception at which parents may meet advisers, members of the college faculty and administrative staff, and parents of other boys in the class.

5. Make important business of freshman warnings. A friendly letter from the dean of freshmen at the time the first grades are published is often much appreciated by parents and helpful to the boy himself. College freshmen sometimes become discouraged by their first grades.

6. Alert the Medical Department to a job it can do. When a student is ill, it is helpful to have the medical officer send a short note to his parents regarding his admission to the college infirmary. Such a note inevitably helps to soften the blow of a telephone call when an emergency operation is required.

7. The dean's office can help by sending an occasional letter to the parents telling them about some of the good things their son has done in the past term, as well as about some of his problems, when the need arises.

8. Arrange parents' weekends. They are invaluable, perhaps the

most effective device of cultivation, and certainly one of the simplest. One or more such weekends will give parents the opportunity to visit their son on campus, and offer the parents an excellent opportunity to see the college in operation.

Williams arranges two weekends, one in the fall for parents of freshmen and one in the spring for the parents of upperclassmen. These weekends feature visits to classes, a luncheon or dinner "on the college," as heavy an athletic program as can be scheduled, an indoctrination meeting for parents, a college play or glee club concert, and open house at dormitories or fraternities.

Registration of parents at these weekends provides a good opportunity to verify and bring the college's prospect list up to date.

9. Send parents' bulletins from time to time. Williams mails picture bulletins, containing pictures of parents' weekends, to all parents, whether they attended or not. The college also sends out periodic newsletters, as well as copies of addresses made by the president and by other prominent Americans associated with Williams.

10. Post the alumni magazine, gratis, to the parents of all students currently enrolled in the college, as well as to all other parents who have ever contributed to the alumni fund.

11. Open membership to parents in the alumni clubs around the country. Many of these hold father-and-son dinners, and dinners for pre-freshmen and their parents. A number of parents who for one reason or another did not attend college are grateful for the opportunity to become identified with one.

After such careful cultivation, how is the reaping managed? The non-Williams parents of current juniors and seniors and of former students back to the class of 1940 are solicited as an independent part of the annual alumni fund by a parents' committee organized in sixteen geographic regions. The whole approach is from the point of view: "We non-Williams parents are doing this on our own because we think Williams did such a fine job for our boy; and we want to make sure that a Williams education will be available for other men who follow."

The regional chairmen are enlisted by a letter from the president of the college. These chairmen in turn enlist city chairmen on their own. The better "pull" they have, of course, the better the results.

Williams follows a rigid timetable which is geared to the alumni fund. The annual campaign among parents is conducted largely by mail. In 1954–1955 the college sent out two appeals signed by the general chairman, three progress reports over his signature, and two regional appeals over the signatures of the regional chairmen. All letters were autotyped, with a four-line fill-in, and were processed on the various chairmen's letterheads and personally signed and mailed in their own localities. All mailings contained a pledge card and reply envelope.

In three and a half months the 1954–1955 campaign produced 472 gifts, totaling $39,064, from 2,086 sets of parents in the classes of 1940 through 1956. The 1956 campaign netted $35,297 from parents.

By official vote of Williams' committee on development, the college does not solicit the parents of boys in either the freshman or sophomore classes. The conviction is that thorough indoctrination and cultivation without solicitation during these two years will eventually produce greater results, in terms of interest in and loyalty to Williams, than solicitation of parents from the time their son is a freshman.[3]

PRINCETON UNIVERSITY

Princeton University's first appeal to parents of students to contribute to the annual giving was made in 1948–1949, when Princeton had to increase the objective to $550,000 in order to provide funds necessary for a general faculty salary increase. During that first campaign, 429 parents gave Princeton more than $52,000. For the nine years 1948–1949 through 1956–1957 the parents' contributions reached a total of $516,000.

For 1956–1957 the total was $70,998, contributed by 1,388 parents. In 1957–1958, 1,564 parents gave $90,543—both new "highs."

In several instances, parents' contributions have measured the difference between reaching and falling short of the goal of the annual giving. In 1952–1953 and 1953–1954 most of the top contributors in the parents' group were solicited for funds for a new Student Center at Princeton instead of for the annual giving, but total contributions to the annual giving still held close to the $50,000 a year level. This in 1954–1955 went up to $60,000.

Behind the achievement of the parents program at Princeton is a reason. In at least forty-five communities, ranging from New York to Dallas, parents not only have made their own annual gifts to Princeton, but have organized local soliciting groups. These are asked only to back up the appeal from the national committee with a letter to parents in the area, on the theory that local endorsement by men known in the community is an effective instrument. Many of these groups, on their own initiative, have gone far beyond a mere mail appeal, and have reached their lists directly by telephone and even through personal discussions.[4]

CORNELL UNIVERSITY

Cornell University has a parents' committee of twenty-seven men, enlisted from all parts of the country. It is an integral part of The Cornell Fund, and carries on its annual campaign simultaneously with the yearly solicitation of alumni and other constituents of the university. Twice a year the Cornell parents receive a special newsletter, "Report from Cornell," along with other publications telling about the university's educational program and opportunities.

The main sales piece is a four-page leaflet entitled "As a Cornell Parent, You're Entitled to Know. . . ." All of the

photographs show students in various learning situations—
in the laboratory, in the library, in the classroom, and survey-
ing on the campus, for example—and the main appeal is for
support of their education, in the service of the nation. A
table on page two makes possible a quick grasp of "Cornell's
progress and the mounting costs attached to insuring the
finest possible education for every student at the University."
Included is the pivotal fact that the additional cost to Cornell
of educating a student over and above tuition and fees paid
by a student in the endowed colleges rose from $117 in 1926
to $814 in 1956. Also included is the related fact that the
portion of the actual cost of education covered by tuition and
fees which a student pays in the endowed colleges declined
from 79 per cent in 1926 to 54 per cent in 1956.

On page four of this Cornell leaflet is a list of nine representative things that a parent's gift to Cornell will pay for.
The range is from $7 up to $5,500 (the salary of an assistant
professor for one year). The punch line at the end of the letter
reads: "Great programs call for great support. You alone
know how much you can help. We can only trust that your
response will be as generous as you can make it."

YALE UNIVERSITY

One aspect of the parents' program at Yale also is worth
particular notice. The chief mailing piece sent to the parents
is an unusually attractive magazine, *The Yale Undergraduate,*
which, beginning in 1954, the university has published three
times a year. The magazine is twenty pages in length, and has
interestingly written articles about "the content and spirit of
student life at Yale." Photographs are used liberally.

The rationale of the magazine, stated in its first issue, is
itself interesting:

It sometimes seems that all mail going from New Haven to Yale
parents falls into one of three categories: bills from the Bursar,

notes from the Dean, and letters from people with something to sell. This magazine avoids all three categories. It is published by the University and distributed without charge to the parents of Yale's 4,000 undergraduates.

DEPAUW UNIVERSITY

Not all colleges and universities which receive contributions from parents get them through the annual giving, nor are they always for unrestricted use. One interesting variation is provided by the Dads' Association at DePauw University, fathers of sons or daughters enrolled in the university. On Dads' Day, arranged annually by the university, the association holds its yearly business meeting, and a luncheon follows. An average of 650 fathers, not quite half of the total, turns out for this day at Greencastle, to share with their sons and daughters their college experience.

The association's executive committee of sixteen men works closely with university officials. Of chief interest is the fact that the Dads' Association works on four specific projects:

1. To provide ten Dads' Awards, valued at $200 each, for students needing financial aid, particularly those whose fathers are incapacitated or deceased. These awards are made by the University Committee on Scholarships.

2. To provide a matching gift of $2,000 a year to the university to assist in maintaining its high quality of teaching.

3. To contribute to a fund which enables faculty members to attend learned society meetings. The association supplements the university budget for this purpose by contributing an additional $1,000.

4. To assist students needing short-term loans of small amounts to meet unexpected expenditures. A revolving loan fund has been established from which, each year, many students borrow from $5 to $50 to meet emergencies.[5]

Friends and Associates

Numerous colleges and universities have organized groups of friends to support specific aspects of their work, ranging from intercollegiate athletics to libraries. Every institution ought to know how to capitalize on the special interests of its friends.

NORTHWESTERN UNIVERSITY

To reach the broader interests of their constituencies, many colleges and universities have established auxiliary organizations most often called "associates." These groups are a sound means by which to develop friendships between an institution and community leaders in commerce, industry, and the professions. Thomas A. Gonser, while in charge of the development program at Northwestern University in 1929, launched what appears to have been the first associates plan. (See p. 78.)

The key to a successful associates plan is service rendered *by* the institution. Benefits follow. As Mr. Gonser sees it, the end in view is "friend-raising" rather than "fund-raising." Although some institutions make membership contingent upon an annual subscription of $100 to $1,000, Mr. Gonser considers this practice a mistake. He cites one institution which, requiring no payments from members of the associates, reports annual gifts averaging $200,000 from them. And the institution has received from former members bequests ranging from $1,000 to $4 million.

Membership in associates groups varies from 25 to more than 400, and depends partly upon the size of the community in which the college or university is located. Some groups are co-educational, although the majority restrict membership to men.

As at Northwestern University, programs normally include

an annual series of meetings at which members of the faculty or outside authorities speak on educational subjects. Some institutions also send publications to members. In large part, however, the strength of the associates plan depends upon a program which holds real interest and value for its members. This plan, Mr. Gonser believes, does not rest on a tin cup. It is based on long-term public relations work for education itself.[6]

With industrial associates the case is different. Each company which becomes an associate pays to support a program beneficial both to the company and to the university which manages it. Two particularly successful programs for industrial associates are those conducted at California Institute of Technology and at Cornell University.

CALIFORNIA INSTITUTE OF TECHNOLOGY

College-industry cooperation took on a new cloak when Caltech organized the Industrial Associates of California Institute of Technology. In a talk before the American Management Association, President Lee A. DuBridge had said:

Whether a company is still in existence and making a profit 10 or 20 years from now—or what kind of product it will be making or selling then—is more likely to be determined by what happens in the laboratory than in the accounting house, in the sales office, or even in Congress or the White House.

California Institute of Technology reasoned that "free enterprise can well aid in the support of higher education and, in return, receive the benefits to be derived from a flow of basic knowledge." The institute decided on something concrete in the way of college-industry cooperation, and the result was the Industrial Associates of California Institute of Technology.

The recent total of memberships has been twenty-five, held mostly by nationally known business corporations. Each member makes an annual payment to the institute (as a business expenditure rather than as a contribution).

The institute now has a campus office for industrial associates, with a full time director and staff. He is the liaison officer of the program and has assistance from individual faculty members, as well as the faculty committee on cooperation with industry.

These services are furnished to member companies:

1. *Meetings.* Several a year are held on the campus. Attendance is by invitation only, sent to members interested in the subject matter of the particular conference. Top faculty members act as chairmen. Adequate time is allowed for the discussion of each paper, and a report is presented by Caltech scientists who are currently investigating the problems under discussion. A close relationship is maintained between representatives of the industrial associates and of the Caltech faculty. Special conferences with faculty members may be arranged through the director's office.

2. *Publications of the staff.* Quarterly bibliographies of publications of the institute are sent to each member of the industrial associates. Copies of any of the publications listed are sent to members on request.

3. *Thesis abstracts.* Members of the research staff and graduate students in the divisions of science and engineering send to the director's office an abstract of every article being submitted to a professional journal. These abstracts are furnished to interested associates. Later the full paper is sent on request.

4. *Calendars.* Advance copies of the weekly institute calendar, showing seminars, public lectures, and the times of final examinations for the Ph.D. degree are sent to members of the associates. Seminars are open to representatives of the associates, and when requested the institute furnishes them with complete data on any Ph.D. thesis submitted. These

theses often furnish early indications of work in progress that has not yet been published.

5. *Library privileges*. Complete facilities are made available to the industrial associates.

6. *General bulletins*. All, as issued, are sent to the associates.[7]

CORNELL UNIVERSITY

In principle, The Cornell University Associates are like their counterparts at California Institute of Technology, but are a larger group. Cornell officially describes its associates as "a medium through which any business or industrial firm, large or small, may translate its natural partnership with a great university into worthwhile financial support, and includes as members all business concerns which make gifts to Cornell under any plan whatsoever."

The business corporations now supporting Cornell through membership in the associates are contributing generally from $1,000 to $25,000 a year in: 1) unrestricted grants (sometimes based upon the number of Cornell graduates employed by the company), 2) grants for specific colleges or departments, 3) scholarships or fellowships, with supplemental grants to the university, and 4) many other forms, including professorships and sponsored research.

During the fiscal year ending June 30, 1957, the members of The Cornell University Associates made gifts to Cornell amounting to more than $750,000. Of the total, $287,561 was in unrestricted grants, and $102,577 went to the medical college. As of October 1957, the Cornell associates had 142 companies or company foundations as members.

In return for the associates' gifts, Cornell considers its most important service "the steadfast production of broadly educated and well trained graduates." Particularly, the university endeavors to maintain good communication with members of the associates through:

1. Copies of research papers, reports, and publications in fields in which associates have indicated an interest. Among these are the *Annual Report of the Vice President for Research* and other reports more technical in nature.

2. Advance notice of university short courses, seminars, conferences, and institutes. An example is the Executive Development Program conducted annually by the Graduate School of Business and Public Administration.

3. A quarterly *Report to Associates,* providing information on significant university activities and progress.[8]

Churches, Religious Denominations

Although more than one-half of the nation's degree-granting institutions of higher education are related to a church organization in some way, the degree of relationship or control and the measure of the churches' responsibility for the financial support of the colleges are not in many cases precise or well understood. However, some light was thrown on the nature of this support by the survey report, *Voluntary Support of America's Colleges and Universities, Fiscal Year 1954–1955,* and supplements Two and Four, published by the Council for Financial Aid to Education.*

In the academic fiscal year 1954–1955, 728 of America's degree-granting colleges and universities received $42,853,747 in voluntary support from Catholic, Protestant, and other church bodies. (This sum includes the value of "contributed services" of certain faculty and staff members, as estimated by Catholic institutions.) Church sources accounted for slightly less than 13 per cent of all voluntary support in gifts and grants received by these 728 institutions during 1954–1955.

The CFAE-ACPRA survey revealed that church bodies in that year gave 92.78 per cent of their contributions to the colleges for current operations, and only 7.22 per cent for

* The survey was conducted by the Council in co-operation with the American College Public Relations Association.

endowment; and that both the Catholic and the Protestant groups gave more than half of their totals for current operations, without restriction as to use. On both scores—contributing for "living endowment" and for unrestricted use—church support of the colleges is significant.

How to increase the volume of that support is a problem which can be solved only by the colleges and the related or controlling churches. In recent years great strides toward increasing support have been made by, for instance, the boards of education in the Methodist church and the Presbyterian church in the U.S.A. The action has stemmed from a conviction of the growing importance of higher education to the country, and from the churches' long established nurture of and partnership with education. The nature of this partnership is evidenced by the following:

1. The American Baptist Convention's Division of Christian Higher Education, Board of Education & Publication, is planning a three-year, $7,500,000 campaign which will be started in January, 1959. Tentative plans call for this sum to be raised through the ABC churches at the time local budgets are raised.

2. The Seventh Day Baptist Church's General Conference now has a committee reviewing the needs of its institutions of higher education. But the Conference makes it clear that each college "is responsible entirely for its own work." Fund-raising is to be handled by each college's Board of Directors, in part by means of college days in the local congregations. One congregation gives an average of $10 a member to support a college.

3. The Southern Baptist Convention's Education Commission and the Southern Association of Baptist Colleges and Schools work together on "a program aimed at the continuous improvement of the member institutions, of their relationship with their respective constituencies . . . and

of the provision for their financial support." Between 1950 and 1956, budgeted appropriations of state conventions had increased by 250 per cent. But no special financial effort on behalf of Southern Baptist colleges is in progress or contemplated. The SBC reports "a definite trend away from fund-raising campaigns as such and toward provision for the needs of the colleges in the annual budgets of state conventions."

In 1957 the Congregational Christian Churches decided that the Biennial Emphasis for 1958–60 would be on higher education. The Churches already have a preliminary estimate that $50,000,000 will be needed to further their work in higher education, both in the United States and abroad.

The Board of Higher Education, Disciples of Christ, estimates that the liberal arts colleges, junior colleges, and seminaries related to it will need more than $150,000,000 during the next 10 years to "provide for, among other things, an increase in capacity for students of somewhere between 25 and 30 per cent. It is not anticipated that all of these resources will be derived from Disciple sources. The development program is not on a nation-wide basis, but will be conducted by each individual institution within the geographical area which it serves."

The Presbyterian Church in the U.S.A. is currently giving special emphasis to higher education, and plans to add over $30,000,000 to its general assets in colleges and universities. In the six year period 1952–57 the Church's contributions to the annual operating expenses of these institutions have more than doubled. At the same time, local congregations have been encouraged to become aware of "their responsibilities to the cause of Christian higher education and to the ministry of the church to the campus." A study made by the North Carolina synod of its junior and senior colleges noted that "one church has reached through experience the conclusion that a minimum base support of 100,000 members is required for the adequate support of a single good senior college. This is clearly established in the history of college financing and operation." [9]

On the whole, it is clear that although numerous Protestant denominational boards of education have a strong "concern" for colleges and universities related to them, the main burden of raising funds from the churches' members rests on the colleges. Most of the funds evidently will have to come from local congregations. All testimony points to the fact that they are ready, able, and willing to help the colleges more than they have done in the recent past.

The Federal Government

Because the enormous taxing power of the Federal Government channels a sizeable part of the national income into Washington, even state governments are finding it more and more difficult to get enough tax revenues to maintain and, as needed, expand the services expected of them. What this fact means to the state universities was made clear by President Harlan Hatcher of the University of Michigan, in an address entitled "Business, Congress, Education—Where Are We Going?" which he delivered in Washington, D.C., on April 30, 1957. Dr. Hatcher's fear was that unless some of the taxing power was passed back to the states, Federal control of the state universities was a real possibility.

The further fact that the Federal Government tends strongly to regulate activities which it supports has caused resistance among many independent, gift-supported colleges and universities to accepting any help from Washington. There are certain types of Federal aid, however, which any American institution of higher education can safely accept. Many applied for and received products left over from the effort of World War II. For example, a Maine college built a spacious gymnasium out of a huge, unused airplane hangar.

Then the College Housing Act of 1950 provided $300 million for long-term, low rate loans for private and public colleges and universities. This program, administered by the Housing and Home Finance Agency with the assistance of the United States Office of Education, makes loans for the construction of dormitories and other so-called self-liquidating facilities. Amendments made by the 84th Congress 1) broadened the program so as to include cafeterias or dining halls, student unions or centers, and health facilities, 2) extended the maximum term of the loans from forty to fifty years, 3) increased the total of loans from $300 million to $500 million, 4) lowered the interest rate from 3.25 per cent to 2.75 per cent, and 5) qualified two-year colleges as eligible participants.

This program did not begin to move until the interest rate was lowered. But during the calendar year 1957 loans estimated at about $290 million were approved. Since 1950 Congress has approved a total of $925 million (in money borrowed from the Treasury Department) for the College Housing Loan Program, and it is the biggest single program of Federal aid to education. On December 5, 1957, the Federal Government announced the largest loan yet made—one of $18 million to the University of California to build dormitories at six of its branch campuses.

Colleges and universities taking such Federal loans are reported to have had satisfactory experience with them. As the Carnegie Foundation for the Advancement of Teaching said in its 1956–1957 annual report:

Although these loans cannot be counted as a major factor in solving the problems of the colleges and universities, they have been unquestionably useful, and even individuals who habitually oppose federal action in education find little to object to in this form of relationship.

Summary

"Other constituencies" than alumni have to be cultivated on the basis of service currently being rendered by the colleges and universities.

This service is unique—the kind that higher educational institutions can give because of their very nature, and can give at little monetary cost to themselves.

Any college or university can develop a parents' program, along well tested lines.

The associates plan can best be developed by a college or university which has a versatile faculty, and/or which is located in a metropolitan area. But it is adaptable to many institutions, including liberal arts colleges.

The industrial associates plan is most feasible for universities, technological institutes, or colleges which conduct extensive research programs and are working on the frontiers of new knowledge.

Official church bodies have working relationships with more than one-half of our degree-granting colleges and universities. These church groups have an increasing concern for their related institutions—and money to give to them. Each college will have to procure it in its own way.

REFERENCES

Chapter VIII

1. James E. Armstrong, "Alumni Giving," *Association of American Colleges Bulletin,* March 1954, p. 101.
2. Information about Carleton's parents' program has been furnished directly by the college.
3. From a paper by Robert K. Hess, "How to Enlist the Support of Parents," read at the 40th General Conference, The American Alumni Council, Bretton Woods, N.H., June 28, 1955.

4. Data on the Princeton parents' program have been furnished directly by the university.
5. From a leaflet issued by The Dads' Association of DePauw University.
6. "Bulletin on Public Relations and Fund-Raising for Colleges and Universities," published by Gonser and Gerber of Chicago, November 1953, pp. 2–3.
7. Herbert H. G. Nash, "The Story Behind the Industrial Associates of Caltech," *College and University Business,* March 1954, pp. 30–31.
8. Bulletin, "Partners . . . The Cornell University Associates," and *Report to Associates,* Fall 1957.
9. Supplements Two (May 1956) and Four (July 1957) to *Voluntary Support of America's Colleges and Universities, Fiscal Year 1954–1955* (New York: Council for Financial Aid to Education, February 1956).

IX

Estate Planning —

Learn to give
Money to colleges while you live.
Don't be silly and think you'll try
To bother the colleges, when you die,
With codicil this, and codicil that,
That Knowledge may starve while Law
  grows fat;
For there never was pitcher that wouldn't
  spill
And there's always a flaw in a donkey's will.

—Oliver Wendell Holmes,
Parson Turrell's Legacy

How to procure bequests is a perennially baffling problem. On this subject one person of broad experience has correctly written: "In spite of tax trends—perhaps even because of them—the bequest field is a fertile one. To cultivate it adequately is not easy. It requires skill, understanding, persistence, patience and energy. It also requires discernment." [1]

Despite the fact that tax rates are high and show no signs of lowering, it is true that both Federal and state tax systems favor benefactions to educational institutions. Government in fact makes itself a partner in benefactions to them, and especially in the several kinds that can be applied to endowment. Since capital funds are of basic importance to independent, gift-supported colleges and universities in particular, it is essential for all of them to organize, and carry forward steadily, well organized programs of estate planning.

Just how essential these programs are is suggested by a glance at the list of college endowments published in the

142

1957 *World Almanac.* Of the approximately 1,350 degree-granting institutions in the United States, only 103 independent and 14 tax-supported institutions had endowments of $5 million or more. A significant fact related to formation of capital is that for the year 1955–1956, forty-nine representative colleges and universities received $40,095,000 in bequests, almost half again as much as during the preceding year.[2]

Calvin Coolidge stated several decades ago that one of the best ways of making a person's name endure is to associate it permanently with an institution of higher learning. Someone else has written, "To make money immortal, invest it in life." John Harvard's name has attained an immortality based upon fourteen months' life in America and the gift of his library and £375 to the young college in the Massachusetts Bay Colony, whose grateful trustees soon afterward called it Harvard. By today's standards that was a modest bequest.

At the other extreme, Harvard has also received, under the will of Gordon McKay, one of the largest bequests ever made to an American college or university, an estate which now amounts to approximately $16.5 million.

Bequests Are Still Being Made

Tax laws now make it difficult for many individuals to accumulate wealth as did McKay, Cook of Michigan, Hall of Oberlin, or Sterling of Yale. Yet large bequests have been announced in recent years, and they give encouragement that others may be nurtured.

In 1951 the will of Hetty Green Wilks distributed an estimated $70 million to sixty-three institutions, including thirteen private colleges and universities and four preparatory schools.

In 1952 Ralph D. Mershon, an alumnus and an engineer, left an estate worth nearly $9 million, and willed most of his property in trust to The Ohio State University.[3]

The University of Illinois in the same year received a total of $912,570 from the estate of a former professor of mathematics there, George A. Miller. Mr. Miller, who while teaching had never received more than $6,000 a year, retired from the university in 1931 and built his estate from the investment of $25,000 in savings.

In 1953 the will of Mrs. Thomas W. Lamont distributed approximately $4 million among seven women's colleges, three universities or professional schools, and a number of other organizations. The bulk of the estate went to Barnard, Bryn Mawr, Mount Holyoke, Radcliffe, Smith, Vassar, and Wellesley.

Also in 1953 Wesleyan University received a bequest worth approximately $6 million from an alumnus, George W. Davison.

Methods of Cultivation

Various colleges have devised different ways of conducting bequest programs. Others evidently leave the matter to faith and hope.

The one fundamental fact about bequests is that an institution wins them on merit almost alone. When a man provides under his will for the use of his lifetime accumulation of property, his principal concern is to place it in hands that he believes will use it effectively to perpetuate some of his lifetime interests. That is a main reason why a well managed, productive college or university is an attractive custodian of such gifts.

Even so, legacies do not drop like the gentle rain from heaven. It is not often that an institution falls heir to a surprise bequest like the one for approximately $1 million received by Princeton a few years ago from a Pennsylvania coal operator who had never attended the university.

The method which enables officers or friends of a college or university to talk on the most friendly, intimate terms with a bequest prospect is the best one possible. In the past, several large universities used the dragnet device of a large bequest committee including as many as 2,000 lawyers, trust officers, physicians, and clergymen. The institutions prepared elaborate bequest booklets for the use of the picked alumni, and placed copies also in the hands of large numbers of non-alumni lawyers and trust officers. But experience has taught that committees of this size are unwieldy and ineffective.

Moreover, it is naive to assume that lawyers and trust officers have many opportunities to suggest to well-to-do people— much less to persuade them—that they make bequest provisions for specific institutions. It is the testator who directs, and the lawyer or trust officer who prepares the will in keeping with his client's desires. So the main target for any bequest committee is the testator himself. That is why the tendency today is to rely on bequest committees small in number, but carefully selected and active, and devoted. It bears repeating that Wellesley's committee on bequests is composed of twenty-five lawyers.

The concern of the bequest committee in any college or university is its long-range capital needs. Inevitably these have to be kept current and prepared in some form for presentation, whether as printed publications or as bound or looseleaf case books made up of photographs, charts or graphs, and accompanying text. Tasteful and attractive books have been prepared in recent years by—among others—Amherst, Colby, the College of Medical Evangelists (Los Angeles), Dartmouth, Knox, Lehigh, Pomona, Stanford, Union College, the University of Miami, and also Radcliffe College for its Graduate Center.

Basic Procedures
Given tools like these, how does a committee best proceed?

The most effective members of it are likely to be those who have already made provisions in their wills for their particular colleges. They can then talk with tact and conviction on a subject about which, it appears, people generally are becoming less and less squeamish. The best way for a college bequest committee to get its program off the ground is to work from the inside out, beginning with the trustees. They have the legal responsibility for the institution, intimate knowledge of its aims and opportunities and needs (or direct access to facts about them), and a moral as well as a logical obligation to take the lead in matters affecting its welfare.

For the trustees and for other members of the institution's constituencies, the appeal, as suggested by Mr. Harold J. Seymour, must have universality in a single common denominator. For the present, as he puts it, "The concept that seems to work best . . . is to urge the perpetuation of one's life-time interests by the capitalization of one's annual giving." [4]

An added inducement, which also may have universality of appeal, is that our colleges and universities must be maintained in strength if our kind of democracy is to survive. As in their approach to business corporations, colleges and universities in seeking bequests will do well to lay heavy stress on the opportunity to help keep America strong by maintaining its institutions of higher learning in strength and vigor. But, as fund-raising veterans have been saying for many years, support through bequests is more likely to flow toward successful programs of education than to needy institutions.

No people should be as well aware of the importance of the colleges as the people who constitute its immediate community. These include members of its professional staff—presidents, deans, faculty members—its alumni and friends, and other individuals whose interest in the institution may be cultivated. In actual practice, as Mr. Seymour suggests, this "working from inside out" method should be followed. And, of equal importance, no one should advocate the bequest program until he himself has acted. These two principles have been well tested in recent years and are sound.

"With such catalytic action," Mr. Seymour declares, "bequest programs will then extend themselves by sheer osmosis, the most vital element of which is effective conversation. Organization and publicity should move *with* the process, and not ahead of it." [5]

Although surprise bequests are announced from time to time, in a general way it is possible to ascertain who, in a college's natural constituencies, has sufficient means that he may be considered a prospect for special gifts during his lifetime and, later, for a bequest. No part of the work of a committee on bequests is as important as that of screening and studying the alumni lists in the search for the most potential prospects. These in turn should be studied intensively: what their interests are, what parts of the college or university and its work may be of prime interest to them, and what member of the committee—or officer of the institution, or other friend —is exactly the right one to take the initiative. This is time-consuming but essential work.

Amherst College, for one, has reduced these general precepts to firm practice. Its committee on endowment has developed two special gifts and lists of about 200 alumni who are believed to be able to make a gift or bequest of $10,000 or more to Amherst. The committee has made a thorough study of the financial ability of these men and of their interests in Amherst, and has worked out a steady plan of cultivation for them. One feature of the plan is a folder of facts and figures aimed directly at the interests of each alumnus in the list. From time to time the committee sends additional information on sheets of uniform size, which the alumnus can drop into the folder, so that he has in effect a special reference library about Amherst and its accomplishments and needs which is always current. [6]

Dartmouth College also has developed a bequest program

directed to its alumni which is probably as broad in scale as any. As explained in Chapter VII, for each class that has reached its twenty-fifth reunion year a bequest agent is appointed who is different from the regular class agent. These agents work in somewhat the same way as the committee on endowment at Amherst, laying particular emphasis on the cultivation of Dartmouth alumni who, on careful review, are believed to be best able to make large benefactions to the college. In its booklet "Philanthropic Estate Planning" Dartmouth holds out this opportunity:

Alumni who, during their lives, have contributed annually to the College often desire to perpetuate their donations and project their philanthrophy beyond their lives. This can be done by creating a "named fund" the income from which will constitute an annual gift to the Alumni Fund in the name of the donor to the credit of his class. Each year the donor's name will appear among the contributors from his class.[7]

In "Philanthropic Estate Planning" it is suggested that after the death of the last known surviving member of the class, the principal and income of the "named fund" may be utilized as the trustees of Dartmouth College determine. This is a clear way of building up unrestricted endowment, and other institutions are adopting it.

Dartmouth is achieving gratifying results through its bequest program. In the third report of the Dartmouth Development Council, dated October 1952, it was related that during 1951–1952 approximately $208,000 was received outright by the college from bequests. As a result of estate provisions maturing in 1952–1953, Dartmouth received $650,000 in additional endowment. Bequests large and small in amount were represented in the total. During the fiscal year 1956–1957 the college received a total of $708,485 from the estate planning of its alumni alone. Dartmouth currently has over

600 known expectancies under its bequest and estate planning program.

Ground Rules

In carrying out any well conceived bequest program, careful attention should be given to a few ground rules which are common to all.

1. It is impossible to lay too much emphasis on the need for a carefully planned approach to a bequest prospect by the person best qualified to make it fruitfully.

2. After an initial call has been made on a bequest prospect, tactful persistence in the follow-ups is likely to be necessary. It will devolve upon an officer of the college concerned to insure that assignments are accepted and carried out fully. This should be one of the normal duties of an office of development.

3. The intitial approach should be buttressed afterward by brief, readable leaflets or other material; and by striking notices in regular publications such as alumni magazines. Here bequests received should be publicized fully.

4. Newspaper stories also should be employed, telling how the idea of a bequest began to grow in the testator's mind; how it matured; and how it was special in the human interest involved. Such newspaper announcements can be used to encourage other bequests. These stories can be timed when the will is probated, at the time the estate is settled, and at the time of any ensuing dedications or memorial ceremonies.

5. All members of the bequest committee should have patience, tenacity, and subtle diplomacy. They have great business in hand. Time only will conclude it—time and the deliberations of the testator. But if the initial approaches are rightly made, if appropriate information is furnished to allow the prospects to decide that this par-

ticular college is the one they want to support over the long road ahead, and if the time of decision is left to them, the college can confidently expect a steady run of bequests across the years.

Colby College, incidentally, has received numerous bequests since, beginning in 1930, it was obliged to build a wholly new campus. The college has carefully nourished bequest prospects. Over the period of more than a quarter century it has learned that, for every bequest provision of which it receives knowledge in advance, there is at least one other that matures.

Methods of Giving

A benefactor of a college may make gifts to it:

1. From income or capital during life, in the form of cash, securities, or property.

2. Subject to reservation of life income or annuity.

3. By a living trust.

4. By life insurance.

5. By will as an outright bequest.

6. By will as a bequest, with life income reserved for survivor(s).

7. By will as a testamentary trust.

8. By will as a contingent bequest.

Bequests During Life

There are advantages in the first method, both for the college and the benefactor. As long as high surtax rates make it difficult for a person to accumulate a sufficient estate to permit gifts at death to anyone except members of his family, there are several reasons why giving out of current income is attractive. Individuals with high incomes can, by taking full advantage of the charitable deduction, make substantial gifts at low cost. Moreover, the same revenue code which enables such gifts will, if an individual endeavors to accumulate a large estate, probably eat up a sizeable portion of it later in estate taxes.

Especially in the older parts of the country, there has been until recently a disposition to build up regardless. There have been numerous instances of men deliberately leaving as large gross estates as possible, as a measure of success in life. In New England particularly, giving from capital during a man's life has been regarded askance. But spurred by current tax laws and personal considerations, many individuals of wealth are tending toward "give before you go" programs of philanthropy. The satisfaction of actually seeing their gifts at work is perhaps the chief among these personal considerations. One elderly New England philanthropist, the late Dr. George G. Averill, actually distributed most of his estate in this way, among academic and social welfare institutions which long had been among his interests.

Other ways of making capital gifts during a man's lifetime include contributing serial rather than lump sum gifts. A man or woman desiring to accomplish a specific purpose for a college can make annual deductible gifts to it, with an instruction that the funds be held until the aggregate is sufficient to carry out the donor's intention. Again, he can name the college as the beneficiary of a trust, which can accumulate annual deductible gifts until his death. A third choice is to name the college as irrevocable beneficiary of a life insurance policy. Annual premium payments on it are tax deductible, and at the end the donor has left a fixed sum to the college for the specific purpose which he had in mind.

By using any of these methods a man during his lifetime can begin to accomplish his purpose of a gift to the college at his death; and he can realize increased pleasure from the gift.

To the extent that they can, colleges and universities should invite and encourage this kind of giving among their alumni and friends who are in a position to undertake it.

The following, too, are all good options in estate planning.

1. A GIFT WITH A RESERVED LIFE INCOME OR ANNUITY

A number of colleges and universities—including Amherst, Bates, Brown, Chicago, Colby, Dartmouth, Pomona, Smith, and Vassar—use this plan. The donor may make a present gift of property to the institution and reserve the right of a life income for himself or any other person, or for himself and then some other person after him.

The amounts required for a life income contract vary, and so do the bases for computing income. Bates College, for example, will draw a life income contract for as small an amount as $500, whereas Dartmouth sets the minimum at $5,000 and reserves the right to make an annual charge of not to exceed one-tenth of one per cent of the principal of the fund for investment and fiscal services.

Amherst will pay an annual income on the value of the contributed property at the rate of return on its general investment fund. Also the college is willing to accept specific securities and segregate the income from them rather than pool the income. Or, if an individual prefers, Amherst is willing to pay an annuity—a guaranteed fixed annual sum for life. This arrangement will give the donor or his beneficiary an assured annual income including, if desired, some return of capital.

A gift with life income reserved has a number of advantages. It provides a method of giving to a college or university whereby the original gift remains intact to establish a fund named by the donor. The donor is able to reserve a generous income for the life or lives of the person or persons whom he specifies, protected by a diversified investment program under expert supervision. Furthermore, under a method of computation approved by the Commissioner of Internal Revenue, a substantial portion of the gift is considered to be a tax-free gift to the institution, which portion is wholly deductible for tax purposes (subject to the 30 per cent limitation). This plan of giving results also in savings on estate and inheritance taxes.

Consider the results which may flow from this type of gift. If, for example, a donor at age sixty gives $5,000 to a college or university with life income reserved to himself, the gift portion available for Federal income tax deduction (subject to the 30 per cent limitation) will be $3,016.05. Assuming that he has a net income of approximately $25,000, his highest effective Federal tax rate will be 66 per cent (for an individual filing a separate return). His income tax will therefore be reduced by $1,990.59 and his $5,000 gift will cost him only $3,009.41 net. If the income paid him by the college in any given year equals 4 per cent, the donor would receive $200 for that year. But based on the net cost of the gift, the donor would receive 6.6 per cent.

When instead of cash the gift is in the form of stocks, bonds, or real estate which have appreciated in value, the benefactor reaps an additional benefit because no capital gains tax is imposed on the increase in value over the original cost to him. Hence the rate of return on the net cost of the gift is further increased.

The donor may choose to select the *reserved annuity* form of gift. In this case, if at age sixty the donor gives $10,000 to a college or university subject to an annuity at the single-life rate of 3.7 per cent, he will receive $370 a year for life. Since 1954 that percentage of each payment which equals the ratio of investment cost to expected return is non-taxable, even after the full cost has been recouped.

In this instance, a standard single premium annuity paying the same amount each year would cost $5,595.14 if purchased from a representative insurance company on male rates. The average life expectancy of the sixty-year-old donor is eighteen years, according to actuarial tables approved by the Commissioner of Internal Revenue, so the expected return would be 18 times $370, or $6,660. The ratio of $5,595.14 to $6,660 is 84 per cent; hence only 16 per cent of the annual $370 payment, or $59.20, would be taxable, as compared with $167.85 taxable under the law existing before 1954. This taxable percentage remains constant no matter how long the annuitant lives, so annuity gifts are an even more desirable investment than in the past.

2. A LIFETIME GIFT TO A TRUST AND THEN TO A SPECIFIED COLLEGE

The same general objective may be reached in another way. A donor may give property to a trustee authorized to manage the trust property and to pay the income, or an annual fixed sum not in excess of the expected income, to the donor or any designated persons for life, and to deliver the property to the college or university on the death of the life beneficiaries named in the trust. This "lifetime trust" is actually identical with the preceding gift with reserved life income or annuity, except that in this case the bank or other trustee would probably charge the usual commissions. The college would not.

The tax advantage of the "lifetime trust" is the same as in the reserved life income or annuity. Subject to the 30 per cent of income limitation, the donor may deduct in the year in which the gift is made the value of the benefiting college's interest. This value would be calculated just as in the previous example.

Such trusts can be revocable or irrevocable. On the demise of the maker of the revocable trust, the principal passes to the benefiting college except for the relatively small tax on the life interest of any third person who may have been named, and without incurring the fees arising from the administration of an estate. No gift tax would apply under a revocable trust agreement.

3. GIFTS BY LIFE INSURANCE

When a college or university is named sole beneficiary of a life insurance policy, the entire proceeds are excluded from the taxable estate of the insured. Moreover, under Federal income tax laws the annual premiums are considered to be charitable gifts, provided the insured does not reserve the right to change the beneficiary.

If, as a man's estate develops, the increase in his assets or the decrease in the requirements of his dependents is such as to reduce his need for all of his insurance coverage, he can make a college of his choice the beneficiary of any policy or policies. The donor gets a tax advantage if he does so, since the fair value of the policy is deductible for income tax purposes (subject to the 30 per cent of income limitation) in the year in which the college is designated irrevocable beneficiary. On the same condition, annual premiums paid are considered to be charitable gifts.

Dartmouth, for example, will enter into an agreement with the insured whereby, on receipt of the insurance proceeds, it will set up a fund in the name specified by the insured, and will pay to one person for life, or pay to one person for life and thereafter to a survivor for life, an annual income based on the average net rate of return earned by the college each year on its pooled invested assets. Thereafter the college will utilize the income from the fund to serve the purpose specified by the donor.

If the insurance is irrevocably assigned, a portion of the "present value" at date of assignment and a portion of each premium subsequently paid are available for Federal income tax deductions. By this method a life income may be assured to dependents which is based on the face value of the insurance rather than on the lesser "present value" of the policy.[8]

4. GIFTS BY WILL

Substantial tax savings may be achieved by testamentary giving. For instance, a bequest to a college or university of any part or all of a testator's estate is exempt from the Federal estate tax.

The marital deduction provided in the Internal Revenue Code allows a testator to leave as much as one-half of his estate to his wife tax-free. Debts and administration expenses, however, are deducted before this half of the estate is computed. Deductions for educational bequests are taken only after the marital deduction; hence a bequest to a college reduces the taxable half rather than the tax-free half of the husband's estate.

Making a devise of real property has particular advantages, for it simplifies the problems of appraisal and the expense and risk of sale. Property willed to a college or university is exempt from the Federal estate tax, so the question of its value has no tax impact on the remainder of the estate.

And there may be great advantages to his estate and his survivors if a man wills to a college or university some property which is extremely valuable but for which there is no ready market. Such property as valuable art treasures, book collections, or undeveloped real estate, which will increase the value of the estate and the amount of the estate tax without providing a source of funds for payment, might wisely be given to a college or university. If a man retains such property in his estate, the tax will have to be paid out of liquid assets. If these are insufficient, the property may have to be sacrificed, at auction or otherwise, for a fraction of its value. Still worse, if the property is completely unsaleable, a man's widow or others dependent upon money from his estate may suffer great hardship.

The administration of a man's estate can be simplified if he gives such unproductive property to a college. He thus limits his estate to productive and liquid properties, and reduces the estate tax to an amount which can more readily be paid out of liquid assets.

If in arranging his estate a man does not feel that he can make an outright bequest of property to a college, he has other options all of which offer tax advantages. Any competent lawyer can advise a testator, or a member of a bequest committee in his interest, about:

a. Life income provided by will to a survivor or survivors, with the property eventually going to a specified college.

b. Gifts by testamentary trusts, again with the assets to be turned over to the college eventually.

c. Contingent gifts to the college. It is always desirable to name a contingent beneficiary, and a college or university is particularly qualified for consideration as such. As a minimum, most alumni of gift-supported colleges and universities could make them contingent beneficiaries when they draw up their wills.

THE CHARITY AND INCOME BENEFITS PLAN

Life-income plans may have, for some colleges, basic drawbacks: a) selection of a beneficiary of the fund is limited because a college must already have an endowment fund in order to have a measuring rod for the income which is to be paid to the donor; b) small institutions with endowments may lack topflight investment managers or advisers; c) income from endowment may be unsatisfactory.

A New York investment firm several years ago devised a new plan which avoids these drawbacks by avoiding use of the endowment fund. The donor has complete freedom to designate any institution or agency as the ultimate beneficiary. He creates an irrevocable trust with mutual fund shares as the principal. Through his lifetime he gets the income from the fund. At his death the principal goes outright to the named beneficiary. Several benefits accrue, both to the donor and to the beneficiary:

1. He secures to himself the income produced by the trust.

2. He sets the investment policy of the trust by selecting the type of mutual fund he wants. He can choose an investment that gives him a high return or a low return. He can have reasonable assurance that his principal is safe.

3. The donor gets an immediate charitable deduction on his income tax return. The deduction varies according to the donor's life expectancy at the time of the creation of the trust, and the value of the actual gift.

4. The donor reduces that part of his estate which is subject to inheritance taxes.[9]

A number of colleges have adopted the charity and income benefits plan as a means of interesting individual constituents in estate provisions favoring the colleges. Here is how it works:

John Alumnus is fifty-two years old and unmarried, with a yearly income of $25,000. If he takes his personal exemption of $600 and the standard deduction of $1,000, his Federal income tax will be $9,206.

If he puts $9,918 into the charity and income benefits plan, his tax drops at once to $6,942. His saving is $2,264. The $9,918 invested in the plan immediately goes to work for him, and he gets the income from it as long as he lives. At his death the principal passes in full, in his name, to the institution which he designated at the time he entered into the plan. While he lived, a part of all he gave was his to keep and enjoy.

While he lived the plan had an added advantage for him. On the $9,918 which he invested in the plan the Federal Government allowed a tax saving of $2,264; hence the gift of $9,918 actually cost only $7,654. In effect the Federal Government added $2,264 to the $7,654, increasing the principal by 29 per cent and the potential of his income by 29 per cent also. In addition, if the $7,654 was invested by the trust in stock which originally cost $2,000, the donor, through the C.I.B. Plan, avoided a capital gains tax of $1,413.

The following table shows the main financial features of the charity and income benefits plan, especially the tax savings afforded: [10]

Age	Income	Income Tax, No Gift	Income Tax, C.I.B. Plan	Tax Saved	Amount in Trust	Income at 6%
55–56	$100,000	$52,056	$38,652	$13,404	$44,867	$2,692
	50,000	19,002	13,884	5,118	22,433	1,345
	40,000	13,354	9,836	3,518	17,946	1,076
	30,000	8,434	6,344	2,090	13,460	807
65–66	$100,000	$51,192	$37,824	$13,368	$34,594	$2,075
	50,000	18,294	13,248	5,046	17,297	1,037
	40,000	12,718	9,272	3,446	13,837	830
	30,000	7,918	5,888	2,030	10,378	622
75–76	$100,000	$51,192	$37,824	$13,368	$28,033	$1,681
	50,000	18,294	13,248	5,046	14,016	840
	40,000	17,718	9,272	3,446	11,213	672
	30,000	7,918	5,888	2,030	8,410	504

Standard deduction of $1000 and 20 per cent of income for charity and income benefits plan gift is used in the figures above.

Summary

Federal and state tax systems encourage benefactions, including all of those under estate planning, to educational institutions.

Numerous large bequest provisions for colleges and universities have continued to be made in recent years.

An institution wins them on merit alone.

Direct, friendly conversations with a bequest prospect himself are the best means of cultivation.

The dragnet device of a large committee of lawyers, alumni or non-alumni, has been proved unwieldy and ineffective.

A bequest program is best activated by people most closely identified with a college or university. When they have provided for it in their own estate planning, the program develops almost by osmosis.

Alumni and other individual friends should be carefully screened by the bequest committee, and cultivated on a hand-tailored basis keyed to their special interests in the work of the institution.

Tact, tenacity, and diplomacy will be required both by the bequest committee and by the college or university office of development.

In arranging his estate, an alumnus or other individual friend may make one or more of a variety of arrangements in favor of an institution of higher education: a gift with a reserved life income or annuity, a lifetime gift to a trust and then to the institution, gifts by life insurance, gifts under the charity and income benefits plan, and bequests by will.

Any competent lawyer can advise a testator, or a college bequest committee in his interest, on these and other provisions of estate planning.

REFERENCES

Chapter IX

1. Curtis P. Fields, "I Give and Bequeath . . . ," *Association of American Colleges Bulletin,* December 1952, p. 525.
2. "Giving to Higher Education Reaches New Peak in 1955–56," a preliminary report from the John Price Jones Company, Inc.
3. While he lived, Mr. Mershon gave the university's development fund $10,000 a year.
4. Harold J. Seymour, "Postscript on the Promotion of Charitable Bequests," private memorandum, March 1954, p. 1.
5. *Ibid.,* p. 4.
6. Information furnished directly to the author by Amherst College.
7. "Philanthropic Estate Planning," Dartmouth College, 1951, p. 3.

8. "Your Life Insurance and Dartmouth," Dartmouth College, 1953, p. 5. This publication and "Philanthropic Estate Planing," Second Revised Edition, are copyrighted by the Trustees of Dartmouth College. Quotations from and references to Dartmouth in this chapter are made with permission. "Tax Aspects of Gifts to Amherst," Revised Edition, 1954, and "Income Annuities and Life Insurance," 1957, are copyrighted by the Trustees of Amherst College. From these publications also quotation and reference are made with permission.

9. *Business Week,* November 13, 1954.

10. Figures furnished to the author by Randolph Scott & Co., 115 Broadway, New York, N.Y.

X   Foundation Grants — "Risk Capital"

> Partners with us to take the financial element of risk from the educator.
>
> —DR. FREDERICK J. MIDDLEBUSH *

Any college officer who wishes to prospect in the field of research or general welfare foundations should take as his point of departure *American Foundations and Their Fields,* Seventh Edition, 1955,[1] and its periodic supplements, *American Foundations News.* And, to save time, he should pinpoint their "fields." For there is a marked diversity in the modes of operation and fields of interest of the major foundations—"the least stereotyped of any organizations in our country," as one close student describes them.[2]

In seeking grants from foundations, the first operating principle is that a college or university has to select its field, and then proceed to work up presentations which will a) advance its own essential aims and quality, and b) interest a foundation or foundations in carrying forward projects of common interest. It is futile to attempt to take a project to market where no market exists. What is likely to interest the Bollingen Fund, as an example, will almost surely not interest the Commonwealth Fund, and vice versa.

It is estimated that foundations reject about 85 to 90 per cent of all applications for grants.[3] In spite of the fact that foundation resources are limited, the rate of acceptance might

---

* *American Foundations News,* July 15, 1954, p. 14.

conceivably be raised if colleges and universities would first study the whole field of philanthropic foundations carefully, and only thereafter submit projects.

The purpose of this chapter is to describe the essential nature of philanthropic foundations and how they operate, and to suggest effective ways of selecting foundations and approaching them for grants.

Number and Kinds of Foundations

American Foundations and Their Fields, Seventh Edition, listed 4,162 foundations on which information over and above name and address was obtained, and which met this definition: ". . . one which is a nonprofit, legal entity having a principal fund of its own, or receiving the charitable contributions of a living founder or founders, which is governed by its own trustees or directors and which has been established to serve the welfare of mankind." [4] If it had been possible to obtain records of all foundations, the editors believe that approximately 7,300 would have been found which met the definition.

SIZE AND LOCATIONS

Included in the category of foundations having less than $1 million principal, or receiving annual grants from their donors insufficient in size to permit the making of annual grants of $50,000 or more, are only 44 per cent of the foundations established between 1900 and 1929, as against 85 per cent of the 2,749 foundations established during the 1940s. Obviously the recent trend has been toward the establishment of small foundations.

American Foundations and Their Fields also reported that in 1955 seventy-eight foundations, each with assets of $10 million or more, possessed $3.1 billion of the total. The bulk of these resources, moreover, is concentrated in those geographical areas where the wealth exists. Roughly 30 per cent of all United States foundations are situated in New York state, and of these 91 per cent are headquartered in New York City. Of the total reported assets, New York state has $2.5 billion, or 55 per cent, and foundations with offices in New York City possess 98 per cent of the amount in the state.

FIELDS OF INTEREST

Most foundations, both large and small, are in fact or potentially concerned with education. Inquiries into fields of foundation interest have shown and continue to show education as the leading concern of foundations.[5] Total resources of the 4,162 foundations mentioned above were $4.5 billion. One observer puts the total figure for all American foundations today at $6 billion.[6] But in 1955–1956 the foundations' aggregate contribution to the total costs of American higher education (approximately $3.25 billion then) was 1.5 per cent.[7]

Philanthropic foundations have the common aim of improving the welfare of mankind through the support or promotion of educational, charitable, religious, or health and welfare organizations. But in their selection of fields of interest and in their modes of operation, foundations are as individualistic as the persons or companies that create them.

RESEARCH AND GENERAL WELFARE FOUNDATIONS

There are research or general welfare foundations like the Carnegie Corporation of New York and the Rockefeller Foundation, old and respected and full of achievement; and the newer Ford Foundation, which possesses the largest capital assets of any single foundation. These three and other large ones like the Commonwealth Fund and the Alfred P. Sloan Foundation are controlled by independent boards of directors and operated with professional staffs. Their grants and their fields of interest are made known through annual or other periodic reports, a practice which is being followed voluntarily by other foundations and may in time be required by law.

It is the exception which proves the rule when foundations like these make out-of-program grants.

PERSONAL FOUNDATIONS

There are also personal foundations, usually capitalized on a much more modest basis than those named above, which after the founder's death continue to foster the interests and institutions which he favored during his lifetime. A notable example is the Cleveland H. Dodge Foundation, which under the direct supervision of Mr. Dodge's son, Cleveland E., continues to support educational institutions in the Middle East, especially the American University of Beirut, and specific colleges and religious institutions in the United States. Other foundations of this type include the Charles Hayden and the (Arthur Curtiss) James Foundation of New York. Still another example is the Cullen Foundation, whose founder, Hugh Roy Cullen, lived to see it operate for the benefit of educational and other institutions located in Texas.

There are numerous small family or personal foundations located in all parts of the country, which because they do not have adequate resources or professional staffs to develop distinctive programs, tend to give subjectively. In general, foundations of this type give in a local area where each is headquartered, or in areas with which the founder or members of his family have close ties. Such foundations give more like individuals than the large research foundations. Some small company foundations have similar characteristics. All of these small foundations—personal or family or company—are potential sources of grants to colleges located nearby.

LARGE COMPANY FOUNDATIONS

A third and increasingly distinctive type of foundation is the large company foundation, created out of earnings to enable the company to help, in its role as a "corporate citizen," to maintain those community agencies and other institutions for which it feels a responsibility. The largest such foundation yet reported is the United States Steel Foundation, Inc., which was established by its parent corporation late in 1953 with initial capital of $12 million. Numerous companies have established or are establishing such foundations, under that section of the Internal Revenue Code which allows a company in any year to give, for philanthropic purposes, up to 5 per cent of its net income before taxes. The largest of these company foundations have professional staffs.

All three of these broad types of foundations, in addition to their charter of general purposes, have one other characteristic in common. They tend to be individualistic, especially the larger ones. Even the company foundations are striving to be different, each in its own way. There is, however, one important distinction. The research or general welfare foundations give in order to benefit mankind by research and experiment in new ideas and methods. Company foundations evidently are going to lean more toward annual grants to operating budgets of the educational institutions with which they are concerned.

Custodians of Venture Capital

Foundation grants, for the most part, do not help fundamentally to support the general, continuing operations of academic institutions. There are notable exceptions, like the grants to 630 independent, gift-supported colleges and universities which The Ford Foundation announced in December 1955. Of the total of $260 million appropriated, $210 million was designated directly for faculty salary endowment, the income only to be used for the first ten years. Also, a few years ago, the General Education Board (Rockefeller Foundation) made endowment grants totaling $7 million to Emory University for the development of its graduate school. In recent years, likewise, three Mellon foundations have made sizeable grants to the University of Pittsburgh. The fundamental aim of all of these gifts was to strengthen not only an institution but a region or an area, and also specific fields of education.

But prospecting presidents should realize that most grants made by the larger foundations are for the support of well sponsored new ventures, "pilot projects" which hold some promise of extending the frontiers of knowledge. The established foundations—the Commonwealth, for example—regard their resources as "risk capital," to be used for special purposes without regard to general maintenance. This attitude has prevailed since at least the 1920s, and is strongly held by most of the major foundations. In his annual report for 1945 Mr. Devereux C. Josephs, then president of the Carnegie Corporation, said:

Foundations do not distribute largess. They search hard for intelligent ways to use their money and are indebted to the wise and skillful who accept grants and do the work. . . . Money is not given for an idea; it is given to a man, or an institution, who has an idea and who has the force and skill to advance it towards a conclusion.

This attitude was spelled out even more sharply in the 1949–1950 report of the Alfred P. Sloan Foundation, Inc.:

The Foundation believes that the funds committed to its stewardship are, in a peculiar sense, part of the risk capital of society. It believes that foundation resources should be used to finance new patterns of action, investigation and research which promise much in the way of cultural and scientific advance but which are not likely to find support from government or from private philanthropic organizations which support well-established activities. In other words, the Trustees of this Foundation believe that if it, and comparable organizations, are to justify their corporate existence and special favors, such as tax-exemption, which the public currently affords them, such justification is to be found in their role as "risk-takers" on man's cultural and intellectual frontiers. It is to be found in their ability to supply initiative and funds for accomplishing the unusual, the untried, and even the debatable, if there is a substantial reason to anticipate results beneficial to society as a whole. Such a policy of deliberately incurring risks can, and often does, lead to failure. That, of course, is the essence of the risk involved. Financial losses which may thus be incurred are to be expected; but they can be more than recouped if some of the experiments "pay off" in terms of the advancement of knowledge and of human welfare.

Realistically, this attitude has to be kept in mind by an institution which approaches at least the major foundations for a grant.

On the surface this attitude, translated into practice, would seem to favor the universities. Staffed with specialists, many of whom are interested in experiment and research, they would appear to be logical recipients for foundation funds. Probably they do get a major portion. In the fiscal year 1956–1957 Stanford University, for example, received $8,132,000 from foundations, of which approximately $1.1 million represented the second half of its faculty salary endowment grant from The Ford Foundation.

Kinds of Grants

Four main types of foundation support of higher education were described in the *American Foundations News* for July 15, 1954.

1. GIFTS TO OPERATING BUDGETS

These welcome gifts are made generally by small foundations established in order to take advantage of tax benefits. Such foundations may be established by families, or companies, or both—with the tax allowance 30 per cent and 5 per cent, respectively. Gifts from these foundations ordinarily are limited to colleges in the immediate area, or to those with which either the families or the companies have close ties. Foundations of this type contribute to colleges which they already know and respect. Hundreds of such foundations are reported to have made gifts to the continuing operations of selected colleges and universities, or to their periodic campaigns or development funds.

The *Minneapolis Star and Tribune* Fund, as an example, in a recent year made grants totaling $15,200 to colleges in the general area of the Twin Cities. Another journalistic giver, the Frank E. Gannett Foundation, has a concern for institutions in the (New York) communities where the Gannett newspapers are published or circulated. Again, the Lilly Endowment, now a large foundation centering its attention on specific fields, began its aid to private, church-related colleges in Indiana with a gift of $1,000 to Hanover College in 1938. Since then, the Lilly Endowment has given more than $4 million to these colleges.

2. SCHOLARSHIPS AND FELLOWSHIPS

Among the newer foundations, student financial aid appears to be a major interest. Of approximately 2,000 foundations on which, for the first time, the *American Foundations News* recently was able to publish information, 10 per cent gave scholarships or fellowships or are legally able to do so. The Alfred P. Sloan Foundation a few years ago initiated a scholarship program benefiting picked students in science and engineering who chose to attend one of four specific institutions. Today, prompted by its accumulated experience, this foundation is extending its program also to selected liberal arts colleges.

Foundations both large and small make grants for scholarships. It is noteworthy that the smaller ones usually grant scholarships to undergraduates of demonstrated ability who live close to the seat of the foundations.

3. GIFTS TO STRENGTHEN THE INSTITUTION

The Ford Foundation grants of $260 million to 630 colleges and universities to raise faculty salaries were classic in design and execution. The chairman of the board of The Ford Foundation made it clear that the grants were intended as an *incentive* to the recipients to raise additional money from their constituencies for the same purpose. This unprecedented gift underscored the fact that grants from the large research foundations—Carnegie, Ford, Rockefeller, and Sloan, for example—often represent "seed money." The older foundations like Carnegie and Rockefeller years ago developed the "multiplication factor" which has now been adopted by certain business corporations mentioned in Chapter XI of this book.

The major research foundations, which include most of the nation's largest in assets, do not engage in palliative giving. Nor do they make grants on a continuing basis for *maintenance*. Mr. Maxwell Hahn, Executive Vice President and Secretary of The Field Foundation, Inc., has declared: "We are looking for transient guests, not for permanent boarders. Foundations want projects with built-in exits." [8]

Some foundations which have large capital make it a practice to give grants devised to strengthen and advance colleges and universities in selected regions, or the institutions attended by the people who established the foundations. This practice is followed especially by foundations which, under the donors' terms, are required to liquidate their principal by specified dates.

In January 1954, three Mellon foundations—the Andrew W. Mellon Educational and Charitable Trust, the Sarah Mellon Scaife, and the Richard King Mellon—announced gifts in the aggregate of $15 million to the University of Pittsburgh. This sum was to be added to the university's endowment, the income to be used mainly for the salaries of full time professors in the school of medicine. In 1949 the University of Pittsburgh received another liberal gift, in the amount of $13.6 million from the Andrew W. Mellon Educational and Charitable

Trust, for the establishment of a graduate school of public health. The Mellon Trust, which is self-liquidating, is interested in developing Pittsburgh institutions to the point where they will give outstanding service not only to their community but to the nation and the world.

Gifts of the same general kind have been made frequently to the Massachusetts Institute of Technology by the Alfred P. Sloan Foundation. (Mr. Alfred P. Sloan, Jr., is a graduate and trustee of the institute.) In recent years the Sloan Foundation has given M.I.T. $1 million for the construction of a metals laboratory, and in addition an initial grant of $5.25 million to establish the school of industrial management. The Foundation added $1 million as operating funds for the school, with the stipulation that the money was not to be used for endowment.

Also in recent years the Old Dominion Fund, established by Paul Mellon (Yale '29), has given $7 million to Yale University for carrying out two projects.

Gifts of this kind often have an added value. If made as "challenge" gifts to be matched by other friends of the institution within a specified period of time, they can buttress the position of the college or university in a fundamental way.

4. GIFTS FOR EXPERIMENT, RESEARCH, OR DEMONSTRATION

The practice of most of the older foundations is to make grants for projects of this kind, not to strengthen any individual institution but to apply to all education. These foundations, with professional staffs in charge, guide programs in selected, specific fields.

In 1936 the Carnegie Corporation of New York made an initial grant of £250 for laboratory equipment to a pathologist at Oxford University. The final result: the purification and development of penicillin by Sir Howard Walter Florey and his colleague, Dr. Ernest Boris Chain. This was probably the most famous, and one of the least expensive, "pilot projects" in recent foundation history.

The main fields of interest of the Carnegie Corporation today are the advancement and diffusion of knowledge through an attack upon specific problems in education and teaching, the social sciences, national and international affairs, and various areas of the world.

On its part the Rockefeller Foundation aims to promote the well-being of mankind through support of significant undertakings in agriculture, biological and medical research, medical education and public health, the social sciences, and the humanities.

The Commonwealth Fund endeavors to advance the welfare of mankind through the advancement of medical education, the development of experimental health projects, international education, and medical research.

The Ford Foundation seeks to aid the public welfare by centering attention upon activities which contribute to its five program areas—education, public affairs, economic development and administration, the behavioral sciences (including mental health), and international peace and understanding.

The Kellogg Foundation is seeking to increase the general welfare through the advancement of graduate and postgraduate medical education, dental education, nursing education, public health training, educational administration, and agriculture.

Another foundation with a broad program in medical education is the Markle Foundation, which pursues the goal of human welfare by concentrating on the advancement of medical education through the retention of able young teachers in the medical schools.

Officers of the large, long established foundations emphasize the fact that projects which they will support with grants must not only strengthen the educational institutions concerned but must have applicability to the entire field of education. The large number of grants made in the last few years by major foundations to colleges and universities to carry out experimental programs in teaching methods and in teacher training, provides a case in point. According to Mrs. Wilmer Shields Rich, these foundations are interested in financing "that kind of dynamic change which is regarded as the very essence of our American educational system." [9]

How to Apply for a Grant

There, in brief, is the field of American philanthropic foundations.

It is off-limits to the aimless or the uninformed.

A guided tour is the best means of circling the bases safely; and some of the foundations have provided guides. For instance, an increasing number of foundations are now issuing annual or other periodic reports. These indicate fields of interest, and warrant careful study. Copies may be obtained directly from the foundations on request.

The greatest single collection of public information on foundations has been assembled at The Foundation Library Center, 588 Fifth Avenue, New York 36, New York. Established in 1956 with an initial grant from the Carnegie Corporation of New York, the center is an independent agency under its own board of trustees. The tasks of the center are to gather comprehensive information about foundations, stimulate adequate reporting where it does not yet exist, and make its collections freely and generally available.

Already the center's collections are extensive. As gift or depository loan it received the related books, reports, and files which the Russell Sage Foundation has been accumulating since 1915. The center has secured photographic transcripts of financial and other data on some 7,000 organizations of the foundation type. Currently it is accumulating information

from individual foundations. The material has been cata-
logued and filed, and is available for use at the center's headquarters.*

But college officials should note well one of the four limitations which the center has placed upon its functions: it will not
advise potential applicants as to which foundation might be
a likely source of funds, nor arrange introductions to foundation officials.

Mention has been made of *American Foundations and
Their Fields,* Seventh Edition, 1955, and of its periodic sup-
plement, *American Foundations News.* It bears repeating that
these source works are indispensable to every college development office. They help to give necessary direction to searches
which otherwise might be casual—and futile. Also indispensable will be *The Directory of Foundations,* to be published
late in 1958 or during 1959 by the Foundation Library Center. This comprehensive work will contain information about
the financial resources and the fields of interest of all except
the smallest foundations.

Now, how actually to apply?

Several of the large research foundations, in annual reports
from time to time, have suggested procedures. The Ford Foundation has made for its own uses a statement which represents
almost a synthesis of these suggested procedures. In a small
booklet entitled "About the Ford Foundation" the following
appears:

Applications for grants may be made by sending a written outline
of a proposal to:
   The Secretary
   The Ford Foundation
   477 Madison Avenue, New York 22, N.Y.
The letter should include a statement of:

* A total of 1,400 people used the facilities of the center during its
first year of operation.

1. The objective of the proposal
2. The methods by which it is to be accomplished
3. The period of time it is expected to take
4. The funds required and an estimated budget in some detail
5. The qualifications of the organizations or individuals involved, and the organizations' eligibility for tax-exemption privileges
6. Whether similar projects have been undertaken previously
7. Whether support has been, or is being, requested of other foundations.

Applications are generally declined unless they fall clearly within programs currently in operation. Each year, the Foundation's income is exhausted through favorable action on only a small percentage of applications.

Please note that, as a tax-exempt organization, The Ford Foundation can give its funds for only educational, scientific, and charitable purposes. It does not support charitable projects limited to local purposes or effects, not does it ordinarily make grants for general operating expenses or construction.

Additional information is contained in the Foundation's annual reports, its quarterly grant announcements, and its occasional special publications. These are free, on request to the Foundation's Office of Reports.

Mrs. Wilmer Shields Rich, editor of *American Foundations and Their Fields* and of its supplements, has published an address entitled "How Foundations Prefer to Be Approached," which invites close reading.[10] A similar and helpful advisory address by Mr. G. Harold Duling, Assistant Secretary of the Lilly Endowment, has also been published.[11] Mr. Duling's address was called "Approach to Foundations." A few of the major points which he stressed are these:

1. Except for grants made by the major national foundations, most philanthropic giving is applied in the region in which the foundation is located. Here is a cue for college presidents. Few foundations are guided by the philosophy of Mr. John D. Rocke-

feller, Sr., who, in establishing his foundation, declared: "I have made my money in all parts of the world; therefore, I expect to give it away in all parts of the world."

In contrast, most of the smaller foundations maintain their interests chiefly at the local level. These foundations, now being established in increasing numbers, may be a substantial untapped source of aid for our colleges and universities. Such foundations are not limited by the major-foundation philosophy of giving "from strength to strength," but can probably be counted upon to have a sympathetic vibration for the small "area college" which is doing an optimum job. They will naturally be inclined to give to such institutions and to the Alma Maters of the families creating the donor foundations.

2. College presidents should call in person at the foundation office, especially in making the initial approach.

3. There is no set pattern for making an appeal to a foundation. If the method works, it is good; and sometimes the unorthodox will succeed. But basic to any successful method is the manner of presenting a project. An oral presentation, by appointment, is a good first step. After further and careful deliberation the project can be put on paper. The simple, concise memorandum is preferred. Fancy bindings are suspect.

The foundation secretary ultimately will need the following information about the project:

   a. The problem to be dealt with and the methods to be used.
   b. The purpose or purposes for which the funds will be used.
   c. The length of time during which aid from the foundation will be desired.
   d. The method of financing a project which might continue beyond the period of foundation aid; or, if the project is a demonstration, an estimate of when and how it might become self-sustaining, or be terminated as far as foundation support would be concerned.
   e. A complete budget estimate for the project. It will be wise to ask for enough money and enough time to do the job well. A 10 per cent for contingencies might well be included.
   f. A biographical statement about the personnel who will conduct the project—particularly about the director.

4. It is unwise to attempt deliberately to by-pass the foundation office. The executive secretary, or executive director, is the chief operating officer of the foundation, placed there by the board of directors to conduct interviews, handle correspondence, procure information about applicants and projects, and do the necessary "screening." Any attempt to go over the head of the executive director may alienate him and antagonize the directors. Mr. Duling adds: "Of course, if you are well acquainted with a member of the board it is quite appropriate to let him know that you are making an appeal, but do not expect him to bring pressure on your behalf."

5. If your request is not granted, it is well to accept defeat gracefully. "On an average, foundations accept less than ten per cent of the appeals submitted to them." There are various reasons why so many applications have to be refused, and the main one is probably budgetary limitations. Another frequent reason is that the projects do not fit the programs or fall within the fields of interest of the foundations approached.

6. Most large foundations are project-minded. They constantly search for men, wherever they may be found, who have venturesome ideas. Like the officers of the Sloan Foundation, Mr. Eli Lilly calls projects engineered by such men "the cutting edge of the perimeter of knowledge." In approaching foundations, college presidents emphasize too much their current operating needs and building programs, and "call all too little attention to the specialties of the star players on their faculty teams."

7. Withal, foundations from their beginning have given support to educational institutions. They are doing so now. They will continue to do so. Approximately half of the foundations possessing $1,000,000 or more in assets have education as a major interest. To it they allocate from 15 to 100 per cent of their available funds. But it is probably a mistake to look to foundations for much in the way of *fundamental* aid. An interested observer has remarked, "A foundation gift is like frosting on the cake, and it should be so regarded."

8. In an approach to a foundation there is a certain amount of luck and fortunate timing. A guiding fact is this: the imaginative presentation of educational needs is the best stop for any gap that

may exist in our educational services. If you have a good idea, hold on to it, market it with various foundations. Some winners have been turned down on the first run, but accepted on the third or fourth and carried to effective completion.

If you miss on the first try there is no reason for not trying again, and again and again, until you are certain that this particular hill holds no gold for your college.

Summary

For the present, colleges and universities will do best to exploit foundation resources which are located, so to speak, in their own backyards. These resources may be traced through reference materials already mentioned, and through the Treasury Department's *Cumulative List of Organizations, Contributions to Which Are Deductible under Sections 23(a) and 23(q) of the Internal Revenue Code.* This voluminous list is supplemented from time to time by the Internal Revenue Service, and copies of both the *Cumulative List* and of the supplements may be ordered, at moderate cost, through the Superintendent of Documents, Government Printing Office, Washington 25, D.C. (A magnifying glass and infinite patience will be useful auxiliaries.)

Foundations which may be approached on the basis of geographic contiguity (or area interest) also may be located by an examination of records in the office of any state treasurer or attorney general. This is probably the quickest procedure, especially with regard to newly established company foundations.

All that has been said here (or that probably can be said) about foundation grants of aid to education comes down to this: hunting for grants in the foundation field requires a special kind of valiancy. It calls, too, for special equipment: a rifle (not a shotgun) capable of hitting narrow targets; a sixth sense that can detect the most likely bushes to beat; an ability to enjoy game that is rather choice than big; a lion's strength defying fatigue; and a capacity for coping with and exploiting surprise—chiefly the fact that the quarry is likely to be found close at hand rather than in the far reaches.

Most important of all: generally, if you succeed, you make your own rules.

REFERENCES

Chapter X

1. Published by American Foundations Information Service, 527 Madison Avenue, New York, N.Y., and sponsored by Raymond Rich Associates and Marts and Lundy, Inc. Liberal reference to the book and its supplements is made in this chapter.
2. Mrs. Wilmer Shields Rich, "How Foundations Prefer to Be Approached," *American Foundations News,* January 15, 1953, p. 13.
3. "Why Business Is Finding More Uses for Foundations," *Business Week,* June 19, 1954, p. 174.
4. *American Foundations and Their Fields,* Seventh Edition, p. 3.
5. *American Foundations News,* July 15, 1954, p. 9.
6. Miss Jeanne Brewer, Director of Foundation Relations, University of Chicago, in "Foundation Giving, Choosing Prospects," Pamphlet No. 1, Development Section, American College Public Relations Association, p. 4.
7. A. Whitney Griswold, *The President's Report to the Alumni of Yale University, 1956–57,* p. 31.
8. Maxwell Hahn, "The American Foundations Face the Future," an address at the winter meeting of The American Association of Fund-Raising Counsel, New York, February 1957, p. 10.
9. Mrs. Wilmer Shields Rich, "Foundation Support for Higher Education," *American Foundations News,* July 15, 1954, p. 13.
10. Mrs. Wilmer Shields Rich, "How Foundations Prefer to be

Approached," *American Foundations News,* January 15, 1953, p. 13.

11. G. Harold Duling, "Approach to Foundations," *Association of American Colleges Bulletin,* May 1953, pp. 329–336. This address was also published by the Association of American Colleges in *Commission on Business and Industry Workshop Proceedings,* April 1953. Anyone interested in approaching American philanthropic foundations will do well to consult also the excellent and authoritative publications of F. Emerson Andrews, of the Foundation Library Center and of the Russell Sage Foundation, especially his *Philanthropic Foundations* (New York: Russell Sage Foundation, 1956), Chapter 7, "Applications for Grants."

XI

Support from Business Corporations

> Today's management must look more and more to institutions of higher learning for the men and women it needs. And to protect the large investment of stockholders, management is justified when it makes the relatively small expenditures needed to insure that these vital supply sources of effective men and women will flourish.
>
> —FRANK W. ABRAMS

Corporate giving is regarded as—and may in fact be—the one remaining untapped source of financial aid given voluntarily to the nation's colleges and universities. But it is well to temper hope with realism, for several major aspects of the problem of corporate contributions are by now abundantly clear:

1. In spite of the acute financial emergency which besets nearly all colleges and universities today, business and industrial companies can not be expected to meet it by crash programs.

2. Making contributions out of earnings is a new thing for most companies, and a problem. They lack "know how." But management is rapidly acquiring it.

3. In their now generally accepted role of corporate citizens, companies recognize a responsibility to help maintain the kind of free society which enables them to prosper. At the same time, gifts which they make are expected to benefit the companies directly or indirectly, and have to be justified in the eyes of the law and of the stockholders. Richard Eells

181

states the matter succinctly in his *Corporation Giving in a Free Society:*

The guiding motive for corporate giving is the *enlightened self-interest of the donor company*. Self-interest is necessarily involved; otherwise the gift would exceed the powers of the corporate board. Corporation philanthropy is not almsgiving. Yet it is distinguishable from ordinary business expense in the sense of operating and capital costs. Its purpose is, rather, to serve the long-range interests of the enterprise within broad social dimensions and thus might be described as assurance or conservation costs. . . .

Through taxation a company contributes substantially to the maintenance of an indispensable structure of public government. The major objective of corporation giving is *to preserve and maintain the vital private sectors in the corporate environment.*[1]

4. Colleges themselves can help corporate executives to deal with the unfamiliar problem of giving to higher education. They can and must present a clear and strong case, as well managed institutions working effectively in their appropriate fields. And they must emphasize the *opportunity* of the company to help maintain the nation's strength by buttressing its colleges and universities, rather than merely their *need* for help.

5. This positive approach will be the more effective if the colleges can say to management that they are already doing their utmost to get maximum support from their established constituencies, especially the alumni. Corporate executives clearly are not interested in covering academic deficits, or in "picking up the tab." The two questions bearing on contributions which they ask most often are: "What do the colleges need (in order to excel)?" and "What's our fair share?"

6. Management's decisions on gifts to colleges and universities are based on fact and not on sentiment. Institutions which, through president's and treasurer's reports issued at

regular intervals, make public the facts about their operations and patently are doing a good job, are most likely to be selected to receive corporate gifts. As F. Emerson Andrews pointed out several years ago, corporations are more accustomed than individuals to get the advice of agencies like the Better Business Bureau and the National Information Bureau, and to require and to study financial statements. He added: "Much good may also come from introducing the new hard-headed giver into a field where sentiment and good intent have sometimes resulted in little practical accomplishment." [2]

Many of the nation's foremost business and industrial leaders have urged upon corporations 1) their moral obligation to support higher education, and 2) the immediacy of the financial needs of our colleges and universities. The literature on the subject is already voluminous, and is growing. In general, the impact has been to awaken management, and stockholders as well, to the importance of companies accepting responsibility for corporate citizenship.

Legal doubts about or objections to corporate giving are being resolved.

Motives of Corporate Giving

It is important for college and university officials to consider the motives and purposes of corporate giving.

The General Electric Company, as an example, over a period of years has clearly defined its rationale for educational aid, and explained its purposes and practices in this field. In a public-interest advertisement which General Electric ran in several national magazines in the autumn of 1957, the company said: "Philanthropy is not the ruling concept. We do not believe it is enough to generate a warm, generous feeling around the vague locality of the corporate heart." General Electric then set out its working principles: 1) the search for a "multiplication factor," 2) the belief that education is a good investment for the recipient, and 3) a genuine belief in education and in the established educational institutions.

Over a period of several years General Electric had a picked task force of veterans in its employ study thoroughly the basic questions: why, how, and to whom? Its study group agreed that to serve the owners of the business, the stockholders, GE's objectives in making grants to higher education were:

1. *New knowledge* through research and competent teaching;

2. An adequate supply of *educated manpower;*

3. *An economic, social, and political climate* in which companies like General Electric can survive and continue to progress.

One other motive for corporate giving to higher education has been stressed by industrial leaders like Henry Ford II. This motive is to keep independent, gift-supported education under private control. The case for so doing was presented clearly by Dr. Harold W. Dodds, then President of Princeton University, during the trial of the A. P. Smith Manufacturing Company case. Dr. Dodds said, in essence:

Democratic society will not long endure if it does not nourish within itself strong centers of non-governmental fountains of knowledge, opinions of all sorts not governmentally or politically originated. If the time comes when all these centers are absorbed into government, then freedom as we know it, I submit, is at an end.[3]

Finally—and not to attempt the compilation of an inclusive catalogue of reasons for corporate giving to colleges and universities—there are benefits flowing to companies from management and labor relations institutes or courses such as Princeton and Rutgers, among others, have established. Also, companies get from colleges and universities such down-to-earth services as evening or extension courses for employees, product testing, and expert counsel from faculty specialists. Management, accustomed to making decisions on the basis of facts, often can get these facts best through a faculty expert's objective, analytical study of a problem or situation.

A number of leading industrialists consider that support of higher education is both an opportunity and a responsibility. For example, former Vice-President Harry A. Winne of the General Electric Company said that it regarded its more than $5 million education budget for 1953 as a "good and profitable expenditure to meet a responsibility which definitely is ours." And in making a gift in November 1953 to the Virginia Foundation for Independent Colleges, President Henry E. McWane of the Lynchburg Foundry Company wrote in part, to President Francis P. Gaines of the Foundation (and of Washington and Lee University):

We are asked what self-interest of the Company is served by this type of expenditure. The Company's interest is motivated by factors that transcend by far the prevailing tax situation. These expenditures represent low-cost investments in the security of the free economic system in which we function, and in the sources of trained leadership for the future. As carefully planned business investments, they promise a substantial long range return. The form of investment has small appeal to the business that expects a dollar-and-cents return to be reflected in its next financial statement. We plan to be in business longer than that.

Who Gives?

That broad gauge thinking of this type is increasing among top management in large corporations is one of the most hopeful findings of a series of studies made by the Council for Financial Aid to Education.

Major national companies have worked out designs, many of them sophisticated, and set examples, many of them excellent.

They have shown that corporation giving benefits those who give as well as those who receive. The author, who has consulted with numerous large business concerns planning aid-to-education programs, has yet to see one go through the ardors without feeling, once the deed is done, a kind of Good Friday spell. The act is that of a conscionable corporate citizen.

It has been performed by companies in all fields. Surveys made by the Russell Sage Foundation in 1951 and by the Council for Financial Aid to Education in the last four years indicate that manufacturing companies probably have been in the van of the movement. But commercial concerns have been joining it.

Companies in other fields—banking, insurance, and public utilities, for instance—have been slower to mobilize in aiding education. Regulatory laws or commission rulings have seemed to some to limit or prevent action. The fact is, however, as CFAE surveys have made clear, that leading companies in all fields *do* have well developed aid-to-education programs.

Some national banks have believed that their warm impulses toward colleges and universities were nipped in the deep freeze of the National Banking Act. *Fact:* a number of banks of this type located in all parts of the country give to colleges and universities. A national bank located in Portland, Oregon, has been helping colleges and universities financially for twenty years. One large national bank located in Chicago has been providing aid for higher education for over twenty-five years.

In a small-sample survey made by the Council for Financial Aid to Education in the summer of 1956, it was found that 66 per cent of the large banks reporting were currently contributing to higher education or planning to do so.

Of thirty-three insurance companies taking part in the

survey, twenty-three—or 70 per cent—reported that they were in some degree contributing to the financial support of colleges and universities.

Of thirty-nine public utilities companies included in the sample for the CFAE 1956 survey, twenty-eight—or 72 per cent—were actively supporting colleges and universities of their choice.

Labor, too, has joined the aid-to-education movement, although most of the unions' contributions so far appear to have been limited to scholarship funds made available to members of the sponsoring unions, or to members' children. However, in 1955 the American Federation of Labor made a large and unusual grant of $200,000 to The Ohio State University. The gift formed an endowment for scholarships in memory of the late AFL president, William Green, a native Ohioan.

Patterns of Company Contributions

Probably the most effective company aid-to-education programs are those in which the *quid pro quo* is broadly based, and in which company interest is clearly identified with and promotes the national welfare. Thus the "talent hunt" principle underlying a number of the largest company scholarship programs seeks to discover and to place in college boys and girls of high scholastic ability and personal quality who, for financial reasons or lack of motivation, otherwise might lack college opportunities.

Some of these scholarship programs are limited to the children of employees—like that of the Ford Motor Company Fund. Others are open to competition, such as those in two scholarship programs of the General Motors Corporation: the College Plan, under which 300 four-year scholarships are awarded annually by 110 private and 68 public institutions in forty-eight states and the District of Columbia; and the

National Plan, under which a hundred four-year scholarships are awarded annually to students who have qualified in a competitive examination conducted by the Educational Testing Service, and who have been selected by a board of outstanding educators. A total of four hundred General Motors scholarships are awarded each year, and when the two programs are in full operation in 1958, there will be 1,600 students in college each year on General Motors scholarships.

Like the Ford Motor Company, General Motors and other donors of scholarships make supplemental cost-of-education payments to the enrolling colleges, roughly equivalent to the tuition charged, in the case of private institutions. The practicality of these grants is that they are unrestricted as to use— the two-dollar dollars which colleges and universities need most.

Similar unrestricted supplemental grants are made in the extensive scholarship program of the Union Carbide Educational Fund, and in the broad national program conducted by the National Merit Scholarship Corporation. More than sixty companies now have scholarship grants administered by National Merit, which was initiated with grants by the Ford Foundation and the Carnegie Corporation of New York.

Companies are aware of the colleges' general attitude on student financial aid—that they help the student more than they help the institution, and may even cost it money. Hence numerous other major companies have sought to provide the kinds of aid which colleges consider most helpful; and companies that based their initial aid-to-education programs on scholarships and/or fellowships have also expanded them to include other types of grants which are feasible for the companies and desired by the colleges and universities. The fact that most of the large company aid-to-education programs are kept under constant review should be of pointed interest to the colleges.

GRANTS FOR UNRESTRICTED USE

Unrestricted grants, so much desired by the colleges and universities, are difficult for most companies to make directly. These grants involve the problem of selection. Many companies find it almost insuperable; they do not know and cannot readily discover what are defensible criteria on the basis of which to give away stockholders' money. On the other hand, most of the large national companies which have full time staffs administering their aid-to-education programs have acquired this "know-how." Among these companies (or their foundations) may be mentioned the American Cyanamid Company, the Burlington Industries Foundation, Esso Education Foundation, General Foods Fund, Kennecott Copper Corporation, the Procter & Gamble Company, The Sears-Roebuck Foundation, Shell Companies Foundation, Socony Mobil Oil Company, Standard Oil Company of California, The Texas Company, and the United States Steel Foundation.

GRANTS TO STATE ASSOCIATIONS

Some of these same companies plus others, notably the Standard Oil Company (Indiana) and Standard Oil Foundation Inc., make unrestricted grants to colleges through the thirty-nine state and regional associations, mostly composed of liberal arts colleges. Through 1956 these groups had received a total of almost $16 million from companies since the first federated approach to them was made in Indiana in 1948. The total for 1957 is expected to pass the $6 million mark.

The Columbia Broadcasting System, through the CBS Foundation Inc., makes unrestricted grants through an annual plan initiated in 1954. The grants are made, on a non-recurring basis, to independent, gift-supported colleges and universities from which key CBS executives, on both senior and junior levels, were graduated. These grants, in the amount of $2,000 a graduate, are designed to "repay" the approximate cost of education not covered by tuition payments.

Still another method of making unrestricted grants is the corporate alumnus plan of "matching grants" devised originally by the General Electric Company. This plan is now used with adaptations by approximately forty companies. It is based on the "multiplication factor" which has already been mentioned in relation to General Electric. This company will match the contribution, up to $1,000, of any employee with one year's continuous service at GE to any four-year accredited degree-granting institution from which he holds an earned degree. Other companies, within specified dollar limits, will match employees' annual gifts to colleges and universities, attended by them or not. The Burlington Industries Foundation goes up to $2,500 in matching individual employees' gifts.

An ingenious program involving elements of the CBS Foundation program just described and the corporate alumnus plan has been devised by the First National City Bank of New York. The bank makes annual grants to colleges and universities attended by bank employees who a) have been with it for at least five consecutive years, and b) have been promoted to certain levels. These unrestricted grants are made by the bank whether or not the employee contributes annually to his college; but they open the way for the college to increase the annual giving of its alumni. A feature of the plan is that the grants are uniform in size, whether they go to the alma mater of the chairman of the board or to that of an assistant branch manager.

GRANTS FOR FACULTY SALARIES

Again, companies have learned that the most critical aspect of financing higher education today is the low compensation of the faculty and staff everywhere. Some companies try to help attack the problem by giving, in one form or another, unrestricted funds. The money collected annually through the thirty-nine state and regional associations of colleges is used by many in the faculty salary account. At the same time, several companies—notably Koppers—annually support professorships in fields and in educational institutions of particular interest to these companies. And two companies in particular, the American Can Company and The Equitable Life Assurance Society of the United States, have made direct grants to selected private colleges and universities, to be applied to faculty salaries. American Can in 1956 allocated $300,000, to be used over a five-year period, in grants to 176 degree-granting colleges and universities, for faculty salaries. A total of $100,000 was given in 1956 by Equitable Life toward faculty salaries in selected private institutions.

CAPITAL GRANTS

Capital grants, including equipment assistance, have been made for a number of years by major companies, even before they had formalized their aid-to-education programs. With the enrollment bulge between 1958 and 1970 to contend with, many colleges and universities, both private and public, will need additional help in expanding their "plants." Numerous large companies are now including funds for capital purposes (current use) in their educational aid programs. Contributions by companies toward library and other building needs are not uncommon.

It is unlikely, however, that business concerns will make capital grants for auxiliary enterprises such as dormitories, dining halls, and service buildings. For these, self-liquidating loans can be procured from the Federal Government, and colleges and universities should make full use of these funds.

Company grants for endowment capital are not regarded favorably by business management, as Council for Financial Aid to Education surveys have shown. Grants for current operations are favored over grants for endowment in a ratio of better than nine to one. In other words, colleges and universities must look to business concerns for "living endowment," and get their capital endowment through individual special gifts and/or bequests.

GIFTS TO UNACCREDITED AND TWO-YEAR COLLEGES

Lastly, companies are taking an increasing interest in unaccredited four-year colleges and in two-year or community colleges. Both groups are viewed as important in the service of the nation, and their opportunities and needs are receiving sympathetic consideration. Large national companies help the Council for the Advancement of Small Colleges in its work of strengthening the unaccredited four-year group; and banks and public utilities companies, for example, with well defined service areas, in increasing number are giving financial aid to the two-year or community colleges.*

How Much?

Among the different types of aid, as has been indicated, the solid favorite with the questing institutions is the unrestricted gift. Large companies previously mentioned in this book, since they first got their feet wet in educational aid in 1953 or 1954, have been the quickest to grasp this basic fact.

The effect of the emphasis which they have placed upon it can now be documented. In the second survey of corporation support of higher education which the Council for Financial

* Colleges and universities would be wise to acquaint themselves with "Aid-to-Education Programs of Some Leading Business Concerns," published by the Council for Financial Aid to Education, 6 East 45th Street, New York 17, N.Y. This loose-leaf binder was first issued in November 1956, with fifty programs presented in detail on a common format. The "case histories" are to be kept up to date, and added to periodically. The book should be especially helpful to colleges to which local or area companies say, "All right, we'll help you, but you'll have to tell us how." The CFAE book shows "what other companies are doing."

Aid to Education conducted in 1957, 275 companies, leaders in their fields, gave an average of 34.2 per cent of their gift dollars to higher education. In the Russell Sage survey among 326 companies in 1950, the comparable percentage was 21.2 per cent.

In the survey of voluntary support of American colleges and universities, fiscal year 1954–1955, conducted by the CFAE and the American College Public Relations Association, business concerns ranked fourth among twelve sources reported on, in the dollar volume of their grants. The 728 institutions that took part in the survey received a grand total of nearly $39.5 million from business corporations, out of a grand total of $336 million received from all sources. Only the alumni, the general welfare foundations, and religious denominations contributed to colleges more than business concerns did in 1954–1955.[4]

Some of the large national companies, from the time they formalized their aid-to-education programs around 1954, have expanded them both in scope and in dollar volume. The Du Pont Company, which began with a fellowship program in 1918, in 1957 expended $1,065,000 through its aid-to-higher-education program. The Esso Education Foundation, supported by the Standard Oil Company (N.J.) and a number of its subsidiaries, distributed $1,332,760 through its regular educational aid program in 1957. In observation of the parent company's seventy-fifth anniversary, the trustees of the foundation also appropriated $1.5 million to carry out a special science teachers program in 1957, 1958, and 1959.

The General Electric Company, which was one of the large company leaders in formalizing its aid-to-higher-education program, put into it $1,348,699 in 1957. Starting at $270,000 in 1955, the General Foods Fund made grants totaling $359,-000 in 1957; and the General Motors Corporation, which announced a full scale educational-aid plan late in 1955, will be giving at the rate of $5 million annually when it is fully developed in 1958.

Procter & Gamble and the Procter & Gamble Fund increased their rate of giving to higher education from $650,000 in 1955 to nearly $1 million in 1957. And the United States Steel Foundation, which announced its first formalized aid-to-education program in the summer of 1954, had by 1957 increased its total grants to $1.8 million.[5]

In every instance, a leader or a small group of leaders in each company brought these results to pass as an act of corporate citizenship.

More Help is Needed

Surveys conducted by the Council for Financial Aid to Education have yielded for the nation's colleges and universities, vis-a-vis corporation support, a number of encouraging facts. One is that business concerns are interested in the welfare of liberal arts colleges and independent universities quite as much as in the technological schools. Particularly the large national companies, with committees on educational aid headed by specialists, have a comprehensive grasp of the problems and importance of all kinds of colleges, universities, and specialized schools.

Another fact, underscored especially by the 1954 survey made by the CFAE among large national companies, is the natural one that community of interest is a determining factor in corporation giving. The companies which took part in the CFAE survey in 1954 indicated that, in giving toward the general maintenance of colleges and universities, they were motivated to the extent of 75 per cent because the institutions were located a) in the same community as a company plant, or nearby, b) in the company's principal marketing area or areas, or c) in the company's home state.[6]

One further fact is also important. Out of a bellwether group of America's hundred largest business corporations (in assets), seventy-nine had formalized aid-to-education programs in force by 1957.

All evidence available indicates an awareness on the part of business concerns of the colleges' importance to them. In the autumn of 1957, in contrast to the autumn of 1953, reports from all parts of the country showed increasing acceptance by top management of a responsibility toward colleges and universities. Now, more than ever, the problem is how to give.

Hence, information given in this chapter is intended to be useful in two ways: 1) colleges and universities may be assisted to come forward in larger numbers with forward-looking educational programs and needs that can enlist corporation aid, and 2) companies, seeing what others actually are doing, may be able more easily to develop well balanced aid-to-education programs benefiting both themselves and colleges and universities in their areas of natural interest.

There are Problems

Why don't the country's approximately 700,000 business and industrial corporations give more than they now do to colleges and universities, and give faster? As has already been said, the corporations—with money available and a generally earnest desire to give where it will produce the best effect for donor and donee—are having to work out a new problem. Its ramifications are enormous, as seen from the executive's desk. Companies have been urged in a pamphlet issued by the National Planning Association to give the full 5 per cent of net taxable income which Federal law allows. Some companies do this, including a number which have established foundations.

But consider the difficulty facing one large company, for instance, the biggest in its field. If it had contributed to educational and charitable institutions 5 per cent of its net profits in any recent year, the sum would have been on the order of $50 million. No executive and no group in the company feels that it has the wisdom to give away anywhere near that amount of money in a year's time. (Not many welfare foundations, with professional staffs on the job, do so.)

Although he is aware that educating business leadership in wise and helpful giving to higher education is a long term problem, Mr. Irving S. Olds has strongly urged colleges themselves to spread the gospel of opportunity and responsibility, at the grass roots level. A hint of how this may be done was given at a meeting of a National Industrial Conference Board subcommittee in New York in 1954. One member observed that "the colleges can't expect the corporations to play God" —that is, to have all the facts and to know all the answers. A second member (representing a large Midwest manufacturing company which already contributes to numerous colleges) lamented the fact that, in his experience, colleges do not meet the companies half way with clear cut proposals or statements of their needs. He added that his company would never give to a college that was not clear on its course and doing a first rate job with the means at its disposal.

So it is wise for colleges to face the fact that companies, in selecting institutions to which they will contribute, necessarily apply merit tests to each appeal they receive. That they *should* do so was one of five major conclusions based on a survey of contribution practices of corporations located in greater Cleveland, conducted in 1953 by the Harvard Business School Club of Cleveland. Corporate executives want to be sure about the quality of a college, or its ability to grow, before they contribute to it. They want assurance that it is already doing a good job, or that ably led, it could with increased financial support become a very good or a first class institution.

There is experience to prove that business concerns linked to special areas are willing to help such colleges located in those areas.

COLLEGE SELF-SURVEYS HELPFUL

On this level, colleges and universities can help themselves and also companies from whom the blessings are expected to flow. Corporations are greatly interested in the question whether specific colleges and universities manage competently the resources which they already have. Every college administrator of course lives with the sound of the eagle-on-the-dollar screaming. But not every one takes the time, or has the special aptitude, for a periodic institutional self-survey. These objective appraisals of methods and operations can be valuable.

Corporations are also interested in being approached by colleges or groups of colleges with the clear kind of requests or programs that will make intelligent giving possible. It bears repeating that they are interested in *opportunity* rather than *need*. And generally they are more interested in colleges that aim to do their jobs better, or on a reasonably enlarged scale, than in stand-pat institutions which evidently are not growing with their times and their responsibilities. Here again it is well to remember Daniel Burnham's admonition: "Make no little plans. Think big."

University of Denver—A Case Study

An exceptional illustration of the reward for "thinking big" has been provided by the University of Denver. In an eight-state area it is the only independent, gift-supported university. Up to 1951, business firms in Denver had been solicited on the university's behalf only once—during a capital-gifts campaign in 1947 for the purpose of erecting a new building in the heart of Denver to house the college of business administration. That appeal was made with the help of professional counsel.

Thus in 1951, when the trustees, in search of new sources of unrestricted annual giving, embarked upon a program of seeking corporation support, they had no history upon which to draw of annual—or even periodic—solicitation of such funds from business concerns. The trustees had to start from zero.

THE TRUSTEES' ROLE

At the outset, it was determined that solicitation of company gifts would have to be made by trustees of the University of Denver who either owned their own businesses or were the chief executives in the firms for which they worked. The professional men on the board were ruled out. The reasons for this policy were:

1. The university felt that the industry support program would be successful only if the business leaders of the city of Denver asked other business men to invest in their great joint community enterprise.

2. It was felt that no solicitor could be truly successful unless he could demonstrate his faith in the project by first having his own firm contribute.

3. And, finally, the university would avoid any unfortunate morale and public relations problems, in the event of turndowns, if the solicitations were made by individuals not working directly in the university.

This policy, when agreed upon, brought two problems into immediate focus. Before the spring months of 1951 the trustees, except in rare instances, had never contributed to the University of Denver from their own corporations' resources. Again, all of the trustees who were qualified by position to act as corporate solicitors immediately confessed themselves basically uninformed about the university in their midst, and specifically about its needs and resources. What followed provides an illuminating example of trustee responsibility and action in strengthening the financial resources of a college or university.

For several months the small group of trustees of the University of Denver who had accepted the corporation soliciting assignment (which grew more challenging to them at every step of the discussions) wrestled with these two basic problems. Their first step was to determine the "fair share" of each corporation—in effect, how much each one should contribute out of its own resources to the university. Eventually they decided upon a rule-of-thumb which would request any corporation or business concern with a Dun and Bradstreet rating of AAA1 to support one professor a year at an arbitrary base of $5,000. Then the participating trustees sought to evaluate all other prospects in terms of a suitable fraction of $5,000 a year, or a suitable multiple thereof, based on a comparison of net earnings before taxes as compared with the net earnings of the four organizations represented by the four trustees who constituted the original committee. Those four firms were well matched in respect to size and net earnings.

The next step was the most gratifying. Each of those four trustees presented to the University of Denver a check for $5,000.

In turn, these men prepared themselves to be well informed solicitors for the university. They were "sold" on corporation giving to higher education, they had backed their convictions with cash, and they were filled with zeal to carry their philosophy to other Denver business concerns. For three additional months they schooled themselves diligently in the necessary facts and figures concerning the university. The treasurer and the director of development supplied them with considerable data on the comparative costs of education. Each of the university's six deans was interviewed at length concerning the specific academic resources and financial needs of the areas which he supervised. The chaplain, the director of the research council, the librarian, the dean of students, and the head of virtually every administrative unit was brought into play to indoctrinate these four trustees not only with the facts concerning independent education, but with the philosophies underlying the need for a strong system of independently supported higher education.

CORPORATION PROGRAM INTO ACTION

Finally, in January 1952, the University of Denver's program of corporate solicitation was put into action. The director of development was made responsible for preparing the appropriate data about prospects, and for organizing the interviews. Appointments for these were made by telephone. Significantly, the interviews usually lasted between one and two hours, often at luncheon, occasionally in a prospect's home during the evening, but generally in his office.

At first the original four trustees did all of the soliciting, as one of a team of three—the director of development and any two of the four trustees concerned. The development officer was present only as an informational backstop. Often it was his duty to follow up the meetings with additional information in writing which the prospect could present to his board of directors.

Ultimately, other trustees than the original four made themselves useful as corporate solicitors. In several instances, donors themselves offered to make calls on other prospects— or were invited if they did not volunteer. Solicitation by a nontrustee business executive was a very powerful stimulus.

SIGNIFICANT RESULTS

The results of this industry support program have surpassed every original hope of the University of Denver. To encourage and support distinguished education there, neighboring corporations and local foundations have contributed to the university these increasing sums for current, unrestricted use:

1951–52	$ 76,400
1952–53	193,741
1953–54	211,682
1954–55	230,725
1955–56	263,928

The manner in which the program gathered momentum and additional supporters is perhaps the most significant thing about it. During the calendar year 1952 a total of sixty-two firms was visited by the University of Denver's trustee solicitors and volunteers, and fifty-one firms contributed. During the first seven months of 1953 all of the eleven firms which in 1952 were solicited but not enlisted joined the university's program, along with seven firms which were not called upon until 1953. In the first half of 1954 the number of corporate contributors to the university passed seventy-five, whereupon a number of holdouts immediately fell into line. There seemed to be some magic in the number seventy-five: it proved that the industry support program was not only permanent, but was truly community-wide. Several donors revealed that they had been waiting for the university to prove this case.

Today the number of annual corporate contributors to the program exceeds two hundred.

Equally interesting was the fact that two or three large corporations did not see fit to join the program until the university was able to prove to them the economy, in their own interest, of keeping it independent and off the tax rolls. (Certain people had occasionally proposed that the University of Denver should be made part of the state system.) With figures supplied by a citizens' group, The Colorado Public Expenditures Council, the university demonstrated that if it should go on the tax rolls it would cost the large industries of Colorado considerable sums of money. One particular corporation asked to have a formula worked out which would tell just how much annually the University of Denver would cost the company in tax support. With the help of the Expenditures Council, it was calculated that based on 1952 tax records, the company would pay $67,000 in extra taxes for the support of the University of Denver. At once the corporation came forward with an annual pledge of $15,000 as insurance against the university's ever going on the tax rolls.

This device would probably not work well with any except very large corporations. The fact remains that it did have a salutary effect on some of Colorado's largest.

THE BREAKFAST PROGRAM

In order to lay its case before numerous smaller prospects in the most expeditious way, the University of Denver has developed a breakfast program, held on successive Wednesday mornings from October through May. A trustee is in charge of this program, and other trustees take part in it. Between fifteen and twenty men are invited to these breakfasts, and all of them—or their companies—are evaluated as potential givers of less than $1,000 a year. About 50 per cent of the men invited have actually attended; and about 50 per cent of those attending have contributed. Attendance at the breakfasts did not decline as news of them circulated in Denver. On the contrary, the impact of the meetings increased as the spring months passed in the first year the program was tried.

The average contribution resulting from the breakfast program was $170, and the university's total income from this source reached $20,000 in the first year. The breakfast program has now been incorporated into a broad scale development program, and still provides an excellent means of better soliciting from and reporting to a number of the university's smaller annual contributors.

IMPORTANT FACTORS IN TOTAL OPERATION

Obviously, the success of the University of Denver's industry support program is due to several factors:

The university does not ask the community for funds. The responsible business leaders of the Denver area (some of them trustees, some not) ask other business executives for corporate gifts on behalf of the university.

2. The business leaders who undertake these corporate solicitations are at pains to educate themselves thoroughly before seeking gifts.

3. The university itself, through its administrative officers and faculty, takes great pains to prepare for the use of its volunteer solicitors a complete picture of the financial needs and the opportunities of the University of Denver.

4. The university makes clear to its friends and potential supporters what it proposes to accomplish with the added financial resources for which it asks.

In every respect the program of corporate solicitation which the University of Denver has worked out is sound, and the chief reason is that it is built on the active participation of trustees. In any privately supported college or university they are indispensable to its new-resources program, particularly because—in view of the high percentage of them who are businessmen—they have access to the business and industrial concerns which control a considerable part of the nation's wealth.

Summary

Helpful Suggestions

To sum up, several basic rules of fund-raising and several particular factors which are new have to be kept in mind in seeking to help companies to develop aid-to-education programs.

1. The case must be bigger than the institution. Today more than at any time in the past there is a potent case for maintaining the nation's strength by supporting and strengthening our colleges and universities. The nation critically needs the best educated manpower that they can produce—architects, clergymen, engineers, lawyers, management men, scientists, teachers, writers and artists, and all other kinds of workers who create and sustain a truly democratic society.

There are two principal reasons why this is so. First, the nation is increasing greatly in population. Second, it must also grow in quality, at a time when events have thrust it into a position of global leadership, contested by an increasingly powerful state which would destroy us if it could. As Walter Lippmann said at a meeting of the National Citizens' Commission for the Public Schools, in the spring of 1954:

Our educational effort . . . has not yet been raised to the plateau of the age we live in. I am not saying, of course, that we should spend 40 billions on education because we spend that much on defense. I am saying that we must make the same order of radical change in our attitude as we have made in our attitude toward defense. We must measure our educational effort as we do our military effort. That is to say, we must measure it not by what it would be easy and convenient to do, but by what it is necessary to do in order that the nation may survive and flourish. We have learned that we are quite rich enough to defend ourselves, whatever the cost. We must now learn that we are quite rich enough to educate ourselves as we need to be educated.

The call to action for America's colleges and universities is to emphasize their vital role in the life of the nation, and to ask from business concerns—as from all other constituencies—a fair share of the financial aid which is needed to keep them active and strong in the service of the only kind of society in which free enterprise can thrive.

2. It is the indispensable duty of the faculty and adminis-

tration to develop clear cut, forward-looking programs of education appropriate to their particular type of institution. Then they must be prepared to present these plans or programs attractively. In dealing with business executives, it will be found even more useful than in approaching individual donors to have clear plans and a specific program.

3. The plans of the nation's 1,800 or so colleges and universities cannot be concerted. Most thinking people oppose anything like a national education authority in the United States. On the other hand, it is possible and desirable for groups of colleges or religious denominations related to numbers of colleges to press for high standards. Instance the Methodist Board of Higher Education. And it is excellent that area groups such as the Southern Regional Education Conference also are active on this front.

In the last analysis, however, the individual colleges will have to present their own cases. These can be made strong and appealing on the ground that strength in all of its parts will alone add up to the nation's strength. We need strong area colleges as well as our great national universities. The local colleges have a national duty to perform in keeping themselves strong, and in enlisting the support of local business concerns in order to do so.

4. Every college and university should carefully list, in order of priority, its current needs for growth and development. It must distinguish *needs* from *wants,* and translate them in terms of *opportunity to serve.* It must be prepared to show clearly what it proposes to accomplish with the additional funds it seeks.

Corporations know what it means to have working capital. More and more of them are finding ways of making unrestricted grants which college boards of trustees may use in their discretion.

For the present, many corporation executives understand

and are sympathetic to the need for new buildings, new equipment, increased faculty salaries, student financial aid, and other things essential to a strong college or university. It is almost mandatory for the institution to have a list of these needs, as they relate to its educational program, and to revise it carefully from time to time.

5. Business concerns will be interested in an orderly presentation of needs and of the case. But they will give in their own individual ways.

6. Nonetheless, large national corporations are interested to contribute, so far as they are able, in ways which will be most helpful to colleges and universities of their choice. Already they grasp the importance of unrestricted grants. They understand the kind of statement made by the Cleveland Commission on Higher Education, headed by leading industrialists and professional people, in a 1953 survey report: "Without unrestricted funds of its own a college or university can not guide its own development."

7. Regardless of its size, any gift to a college from a business concern should be acknowledged. Also, it gratifies any donor to know what the recipient institution has been able to do with a contribution which it might otherwise have been unable to do. A working relationship based on mutual confidence and understanding is an excellent thing for a college and for a company. Colleges need have no fear of intrusion in their internal affairs. The men who administer aid-to-education programs, especially for the large national companies, are of top quality. Many colleges have discovered that in these men they have good friends.

8. Not to be overlooked is the need to have strong, or stronger, laws passed by state legislatures to permit corporations to make educational and charitable gifts. Through 1957 a total of at least forty states and Hawaii had passed such laws. Some were put forward by educational institutions, as in Louisiana and in the six New England states. In Ohio and

Indiana, college foundations were instrumental in having permissive laws already on the statute books broadened to enable more corporations to give—especially banks, insurance companies, and public utilities.

Legal counsel in some cases is still wary and conservative on the subject of corporation contributions to higher education. Nothing could help better to clear the way for a general participation by companies in support of higher education than clear cut statutes of the kind which have been passed by, for example, the legislatures of Rhode Island and Virginia in 1952 and 1953 respectively.

9. An inducement to companies to give financial support for higher education is the need for colleges to put tremendous stress on *investment in men*—in the faculties of colleges and universities.* Facts and figures are available to show that teachers—and especially college teachers—are the one professional class which has not been permitted to share in the economic prosperity of the United States in the last twelve to fifteen years. Corporation executives do not all know, but urgently need to be told, that the men and women who are teaching their children in colleges and universities all across the land are being exploited by the wealthiest nation in the world.

Look at it another way. A scholarship gift by a company may help a boy or girl. A gift that enables a college to develop and hold a first class professor helps hundreds of students, year after year. Here is the best "multiplication factor" of all. This is a fact to impress upon business concerns, which could not exist except for the men with ideas and initiative and other special talents who can be trained up for the key jobs in management.

Charles W. Eliot, when inaugurated as President of Harvard

* A useful tool might be a staff study, "Backing Up Brains," published by the Council for Financial Aid to Education in November 1957.

in 1869, made a classic statement on the pivotal importance of the faculty in an institution of higher learning. He said:

The University as a place of study and instruction is, at any moment, what the Faculties make it. The professors, lecturers, and tutors of the University are the living sources of learning and enthusiasm. They personally represent the possibilities of instruction. . . . As a fact, progress comes mainly from the Faculties.[7]

REFERENCES

Chapter XI

1. Richard Eells, *Corporation Giving in a Free Society* (New York: Harper & Brothers, 1956), pp. 136, 137.
2. F. Emerson Andrews, "New Giant in Giving: Big Business," *New York Times Sunday Magazine,* December 2, 1951, p. 36.
3. Supreme Court of New Jersey, No. A–160, September term, 1952. A. P. Smith Manufacturing Company vs. Ruth F. Barlow, pp. 3–4.
4. See *Voluntary Support of America's Colleges and Universities: Survey of the Sources, Volume, and Purposes of Gifts and Grants Received During the Fiscal Year 1954–55* (New York: Council for Financial Aid to Education, Inc., February 1956).
5. These and similar data in this chapter have been furnished to the Council for Financial Aid to Education by the companies concerned, with publication authorized.
6. *Institutional Needs in Higher Education and Corporation Practices in Aid: Summary Results of Two Questionnaire Surveys Conducted During 1954* (New York: Council for Financial Aid to Education, June 1955), *passim.*
7. Charles W. Eliot, *Educational Reform* (New York: The Century Co., 1898), p. 24.

XII

The Community and the College

Charity begins at home, is the voice of the world.

—SIR THOMAS BROWNE,
Religio Medici

In both a geographic and cultural sense, a college or university is inevitably a part of the community in which it is situated. Also inevitably, each aids the other. They live together on a two-way street.

A college does well to realize that although charity begins at home, so does service. There are several kinds of service which a college or university is uniquely able to render. Woodrow Wilson, in 1909, still president of Princeton and three years away from the White House, defined the most important services in these terms:

The college of the ideal American university, therefore, is a place intended for general intellectual discipline and enlightenment; and not for intellectual discipline and enlightenment only, but also for moral and spiritual discipline and enlightment. America is great, not by reason of her skill, but by reason of her spirit of general serviceableness and intelligence. That is the reason why it is necessary to keep her colleges under constant examination and criticism. If we do not they may forget their true function, which is to supply America and the professions with enlightened men.[1]

Wilson's last sentence touches the nub of the problem of good college-community relations. When alumni pressure groups, or business concerns or executives, or Chambers of

209

Commerce, or American Legion posts undertake to tell the colleges what kinds of subjects they should teach and who should do the teaching, bad relations are in the making. And if the colleges acquiesce and submit to the pressures, trouble is assured. That is why the dignified and courageous stands taken in recent years by Presidents Harold Taylor of Sarah Lawrence and Nathan Pusey of Harvard—to name only two academic heads—have shown the would-be interlopers to be as negligible as they are, and have added new strength to the old truth that the legal responsibility for colleges and universities rests with their governing boards, and the operational responsibility with their administrative officers and faculties. Mr. Pusey and Mr. Taylor have demonstrated anew a sovereign principle of good relations between college and community. Getting along amicably depends in good part on a college's resistance to any threat of outside interference in its internal affairs.

Another main service of institutions of higher education was indicated by Abraham Flexner, who in 1930 wrote:

. . . a university, like all other human institutions—like the church, like governments, like philanthropic organizations—is not outside, but inside the general social fabric of a given era. It is not something apart, something historic, that yields as little as possible to forces and influences that are more or less new. It is, on the contrary . . . an expression of the age, as well as an influence operating upon both present and future.[2]

In the intervening years, town and gown have come closer together. Mutual understanding has grown, in spite of occasional pinpricks here and there—as in the spring, when winter-suppressed undergraduate steam erupts in incalculable ways and directions.

Actual ways in which town and gown co-operate have been summarized in a report published by the New York State Citizens Council, the Association of Colleges and Univer-

sities of New York, and the State University of New York.[3]
Four methods stand out:

1. Use by the college of the skills, abilities, and education
of persons within the community for the purpose of enriching
this educational process.

2. Use by the college of the community as a laboratory for
the purpose of advancing the educational process.

3. Initiation by the college of various community undertakings in which the college functions merely as one of the
agencies within the community.

4. Development by college and community of mutually
beneficial undertakings.

At Fordham University, for example, these methods are
used in various ways in a well devised college-community
program. The university's faculty carries on research for local,
state, and national governmental and welfare agencies. These
projects have involved such programs as an investigation of
stream pollution in Westchester County, work with the director of the botanical gardens in the Bronx, seismological research under the auspices of the city of New York, smoke
control, first-aid training, problems of young people, and use
of the lie detector.

In Boston, Northeastern University has a carefully devised
service-to-the-community program. During 1954–1955, for
instance, Northeastern made its facilities available to business
and industry, to local and Federal governments, to the armed
forces, and to other agencies. Community service projects
included several which originated in the university's Bureau
of Business and Economic Research. The bureau has continued to attract much favorable attention to Northeastern
through "the practical and down-to-earth investigations conducted."

A report on displaced textile workers, prepared by the
director and staff, received national recognition. Current or

recent investigations, such as those concerning "The Economics of Employing the Older Worker," "Cycles and Trends in the American Cotton Textile Industry," and "The Economics of Freezing Fish at Sea," were undertaken to assist both industry and government in economic planning.

Planning a Program

Any college or university has or can develop areas of community service. Cultivating them will, in good season, bring to the institution the understanding and support which it must have in order to exist.

As a beginning, it is essential to discover what services its "publics" want and the college or university can appropriately render. It will do positive harm rather than good to give these publics what the institution thinks they *need* rather than what they want. These groups include, for example, local alumni, suppliers, local students living off campus and their parents, prospective local students and their parents, social and fraternal groups, business and professional organizations, non-alumni friends, and just the man in the street. All of these publics are external to the college.

An advisory committee of opinion leaders carefully selected from among these groups can be helpful both to the college and to the community. Many colleges have developed and worked with such committees, on which college officers—both administrative and faculty—and students can serve with good effect. Such committees can and do help colleges to develop community outreach and intake. Their whole endeavor is based on interpretation. And they proceed on the principle that action is more effective than words.

Nearly any institution of higher education can find ample opportunities for interpretation by taking the campus to the community. A mayor may be confronted with a problem that can be moved toward solution by a community survey—which students in the social sciences, accounting, or statistics might conduct as a study project. Boys' clubs profit by the interest and help of college students.

Colleges do well, also, to attract the community to the campus. Various approved clubs could make excellent use of certain college facilities when they are not at work for the college. Colby College, for instance, has a broad series of summer institutes, ranging from tax accounting to ophthalmology, which draw men and women from all over the country to the Mayflower Hill campus. Every one of these business and professional people is a potential friend of Colby. And the institutes pay their way.

The college-community advisory committee could start simply by exploring questions like these:

Can the college library broaden the resources of the community library?

Are members of the faculty able to contribute to any local venture in adult education?

Are the college's facilities for art, music, drama, and the dance of the sort to enrich community life?

Are there lectures on varied topics which the college arranges or could arrange to which the public might wish to come, on invitation?

Are faculty members active in the community—or is it always the president or the dean who makes the public appearances?

Is there any validity to the charge that the institution is aloof? [4]

Communities generally are eager to be proud of local institutions. A college or university has, in its own locality, almost a first claim on the community's goodwill. The institution can cement this goodwill by intelligent planned action.

Nothing it can do contributes more effectively to that end than a well conceived "open house." During American Education Week in the autumn of 1954, a number of colleges and universities all over the country for the first time invited their publics in to see the institution at work. Harvard University has been among the number to employ this device, and with most gratifying results. Displays, demonstrations, informal talks by president or dean, and firsthand contact with students are among the main ingredients of the formula.

One well known development officer underscores the importance of enlisting the active interest of local alumni in college-community programs. Dr. T. W. Van Arsdale, Jr., while director of development at the University of Buffalo, remarked that amidst variables, in local situations, there was always one constant factor: "the alumni—forever present, already indoctrinated, and potentially so effective."

A few years ago the University of Buffalo made the Annual Participating Fund for Medical Education an entity separate from the alumni loyalty fund. A soliciting organization was created, and medical school alumni as well as non-alumni physicians practicing in Buffalo and its immediately surrounding area were asked to pledge a minimum of $100 a year. By 1955 a total of 92 per cent of all these physicians had made the basic pledge. The annual participating fund has received local and national publicity. Local citizens began to inquire about the fund. In chance encounters, committee members began to be asked how lay citizens might pledge to it.

One day a member of the committee received an inquiry about the fund from a patient. Once he had the facts, the patient changed his will. On his death in the spring of 1955 the university received a bequest from his estate in the amount of $10 million.[5]

Methods of Local Solicitation

Some of the charity going to a college from its community

will flow in naturally. Most of it, however, as in all other areas of college fund-raising, will be procured by organized solicitation. Two instances will suggest "how-to" methods and procedures.

HASTINGS COLLEGE

Consider, first, Hastings College, a co-educational institution with an enrollment of about 725 students. It is located in the Nebraska community for which it is named, and is described as "Hastings' No. 1 Civic Asset." The college considers its procedure in the community campaign as "fairly simple." First of all, the college attempts to create "an intelligent and favorable climate of opinion." Hastings tells its story by means of 1) printed material placed in the hands of every conceivable group, 2) newspaper publicity, and 3) speakers from the college in the fifteen churches of the community on the Sunday preceding Hastings College Day.

The next step is the organization of a special gifts committee of around sixty people. They call upon about three hundred potential donors from whom the college expects to get about 80 per cent of the quota. Next are enlisted approximately three hundred workers who will see perhaps nine hundred people other than themselves during the one day solicitation. The college tries to have the work of the special gifts committee completed *before* the one day solicitation, which starts with a breakfast and ends with a dinner on the same day.

In 1955 the college asked the community of Hastings, with 20,000 souls, to give $30,000 for the college's current operations. The community actually gave the college a little more than $40,000.

Only one "sales piece" was printed for Hastings College's 1955 community campaign—a two-color, four-page leaflet in size 8½ x 11 inches. In capsule form the college explained its case: the nature of its service to Hastings and to the nation, the reason why it needs gift income, how much of it was needed to balance the college's budget, where the gift income would have to come from, and how Hastings' needs for operating funds compare with those of comparable colleges.

Implicit in the sales argument of the campaign leaflet are the two points referred to earlier in this chapter, which were made by Woodrow Wilson and Abraham Flexner. Hastings' marshaling of facts may be of use to other colleges in their community appeals:

Hastings College was founded in 1882—73 years of continuous service.

Hastings College's physical plant and endowment are valued at more than $2,000,000.

Hastings College spends $550,000 annually in Hastings.

236 local students each year have top college experience *at home.*

236 local students spend their tuition and maintenance in Hastings instead of taking it out of town. (236 x $320, tuition alone, is $75,520 kept here every year in addition to living expenses for 236 students.)

Families of students and friends from outside of Hastings bring thousands of dollars into Hastings annually *in addition to fees and tuition* paid through the college.

Every dollar *given* to Hastings College by Hastings citizens *is matched by* a dollar *given* by friends outside Hastings.

Every dollar *given* to Hastings College returns tenfold in Hastings' trade channels.

897 alumni live in the Hastings trade territory, raising living standards—raising cultural standards.

Hastings is known far and wide as the home of Hastings College, an outstanding Christian [Presbyterian] college.

Students from 38 States, the District of Columbia, and 18 foreign countries have attended Hastings College.

In advance of the dawn-to-dusk day of solicitation, April 20, Hastings gave careful attention to organization. It stemmed naturally from the steering committee, the finance committee of the board of trustees. Below it in the organization chart was the planning committee of fifteen to twenty-five citizens, and then the general chairmen in charge of three operating committees: big gifts (three divisions), promotion and publicity (three subcommittees), and general solicitation (six divisions). On the average, each of 216 workers in the general solicitation had about five cards.

The big gifts committee had twelve teams of five members each, including a captain who was made responsible for enlisting the other four men. This committee had a kick-off breakfast on March 30, and weekly report breakfasts thereafter until the day of solicitation. The captains were encouraged in their work by mimeographed bulletins issued in the three-week period of big gifts solicitation; for, as in all well managed campaigns, emphasis was placed on selection. The planning committee had a realistic concept of the scale of giving required to produce $36,500:

Number	Amount	Total
4	$2,500	$10,000
2	1,500	3,000
8	1,000	8,000
10	500	5,000
12	250	3,000
36		29,000
250	(average) 30	7,500
		$36,500

As has been stated, the campaign committee as a whole raised a bit more than $40,000 for Hastings College in 1955. By April 13, one week before the day of solicitation, the big gifts committee had in hand $21,000 of its $28,000 quota.[6]

PARSONS COLLEGE

Parsons College, like Hastings, is co-educational, but a few years older and nearly 50 per cent smaller. Its student body is reported as 512. Parsons is located in Fairfield, Iowa, population 7,300 in 1950.

Parsons' experience proves that a home town can be a potent and permanent factor in financing a college. The Fairfield Fund for Parsons College, organized in 1944, functions much like a one-agency community chest. The fund supplies vital financial support, but in addition has become a prime factor in ideal college-community relations.

In the nine-year period 1944–1952 the fund channeled an average of $25,000 a year into the college's $300,000 operating budget—all in unrestricted funds. About 90 per cent of the contributions were made in cash, and the remainder in pledges has rarely shown any shrinkage on collection.

In 1952 the Fairfield Fund for Parsons College set new records as a single-day community drive in November. The fund exceeded its goal by more than $1,000, was supported by more than 450 business concerns and individuals, and attracted 150 new givers—a 50 per cent increase.

The initial organization of the fund in 1944 was spurred by the receipt of sizeable gifts from outsiders, whose direct gain was far less than that of the community. Set on its way by a nucleus of leading citizens of Fairfield with the boost of a challenge gift from outside, the Fairfield Fund in its first year totaled $14,000. In 1948 it first reached the $25,000 level.

Parsons' president and staff act as campaign directors. But the fund has been most successful since volunteer citizens were organized into soliciting teams. No member calls on more than six or seven prospects. Individual gifts have ranged from one of $3,000 to eight for $1 each.

Soliciting is done by two divisions: the general division, which seeks gifts in the range of $1 to $50; and the special gifts division, whose target is gifts of more than $50. An impartial and confidential evaluation committee sets suggested amounts for each firm and individual prospect. From a total prospect list of 675, more than 460 contributions were obtained during 1952 by a working organization of 130 volunteers.

Intelligent follow-up of the annual campaign includes an attractive personal report to all workers and to contributors of $50 or more; a personal thank-you letter from Parsons' president to every giver; and year-round attention to all local public relations aspects of the college in its community.

To Parsons College the results of the annual local campaign have greater significance than mere dollars and cents:

1. Local citizens express a real participant's interest in the affairs of the college.

2. As proud participants in financing the college, Fairfield citizens become enthusiastic advocates outside the community.

3. Local citizens gain an intelligent understanding of the college's aims and problems.

4. Local young people are better aware of the opportunities offered them in the home town college.

The community, too, benefits in various ways from the Fairfield Fund for Parsons College:

1. Established as an annual program, the Fairfield Fund is included in most individuals' annual contributions budgets, and is not regarded as the usual irksome begging.

2. The college is constantly on its toes to be a better citizen itself and to retain the community's confidence.

3. Many extra educational services are offered readily as a result of the community's support.

4. The college is a better community asset in attracting new business and good citizens.

5. Because of local support, outsiders were more inclined to help underwrite a $360,000 development program in 1953, including new buildings and educational improvements.

The 1953 campaign of the Fairfield Fund for Parsons College had a goal of $25,000. There was a volunteer chairman and also a campaign chairman. Preparatory letters to prospective solicitors emphasized such points as:

1. An investment in Parsons returns $11 on each investment of $1 (1,100 per cent return).

2. Over $280,000 of the college's $307,742 budget is spent locally for salaries, utilities, services, materials and labor, not including students' and visitors' expenditures of more than $100,000 a year.

3. Friends of Parsons outside of Fairfield increased their annual support from $15,000 to more than $123,000 in the period 1944–1953.

The operating plan of the Fairfield Fund was similar to that of its counterpart in Hastings. The leadership gifts committee had the period November 3 to 17 in which to complete solicitation of its prospects. Cards for them were given out at a called meeting. There was a regular schedule of publicity events and releases.

On November 17 there was a kick-off breakfast, which lasted only from 7:30 to 8:10, and a report and tally meeting was held on the evening of the same day.

Average gifts during the decade to the Fairfield Fund for Parsons College were:

Professional ......$132   (range: $30 to $500)
Retail ....$162   (range: $25 to $300)
Services ....$183   (range: $100 to $400) [7]

Summary

A college and the community in which it is situated live together on a two-way street.

The college does well to remember that although charity begins at home, so does service.

In rendering service to the community, the college must control its own fate and cling to its main function, which is to help supply America and the professions with enlightened men and women.

College-community relations are varied; they can enrich both partners.

A college does well to consider carefully how it may best serve the community. Cultivating areas of community service appropriate to it will in season bring to the college the understanding and support which are essential to its existence.

REFERENCES

Chapter XII

1. Woodrow Wilson, *College and State: Educational, Literary and Political Papers, 1875–1913* ed. by Ray Stannard Baker and William E. Dodd (New York and London: Harper & Brothers, 1925), Vol. II, pp. 149–150.
2. Abraham Flexner, *Universities, American, English, German* (New York, London, Toronto: Oxford University Press, 1930), p. 3.
3. H. Curtis Mial, *College-Community Relationships in New York State (A Report of Activities in Twenty-six Colleges and Universities),* December 1953.
4. David M. Church, "Interpretation of Higher Education to the Community—A Shared Responsibility," paper presented before the Eleventh National Conference on Higher Education, Association for Higher Education, Chicago, March 6, 1956, p. 6, *passim.*
5. T. W. Van Arsdale, Jr., "How to Use Alumni in Developing Community Support," *The "How to" of Educational Fund Raising* (Washington, D.C., The American Alumni Council, January 1956), p. 92. Also worth perusal is the preceding article (pp. 84–91) in the same publication, "How to Obtain Financial Support from the Local Community," by Thomas P. Nickell, University of Southern California.
6. Information about Hastings College was furnished to the author by President Dale D. Welch in a letter of January 26, 1956.

7. Information about Parsons College was furnished to the author by the College. Some of it appears in an article by Walter W. Reed, "Don't Overlook Gifts from the Town," in *Trustee,* a quarterly letter to trustees of church-related institutions of higher learning, published by the Commission on Higher Education, National Council of Churches of Christ in the U.S.A., October 1953.

XIII   Conducting A Mail Appeal

She wooes you by a figure.—What figure?
—By letter, I should say.

—Two Gentlemen of Verona

Every approach to every member of a college's total constituency should be made on the level of important business. Experience has shown that no card in the game of college fundraising is as effective as personal solicitation. As a matter of practice then, in annual giving as in a capital-gifts campaign, prospects rated as having the greatest financial ability should receive the "personal touch." On the other hand, reaching the largest number of prospects, or marginal possibilities, calls for the use of mail.

Selling by mail is difficult. Volumes have been written about it, and are accessible in any good library. Our concern here is with selling the cause of a college or university by mail, and this matter has special aspects which are not common to selling by mail in general.

The total constituency of a college or university is "fit though few." All that the institution can muster of skill and taste and intelligence is needed to cultivate it. Each institution has its own personality, or "tone," and is different from every other. Any letter or mailing piece sent by the college should be its personal ambassador. It should be distinctive, in the way that bulletins and other publications of Bowdoin College, Carnegie Institute of Technology, Massachusetts Institute of Technology, and the University of Pennsylvania are not only distinctive but distinguished. The list could be extended (but not far) both for publications and for letterheads.

The Language of Request

Even more important is what David McCord, Executive Secretary of the Harvard Fund, calls "the language of request." [1] He has said:

As I look over the selected quantity of our promotional material which, like all of you, I scan from month to month, how very few pieces seem really to suggest in tone or language or typography the image of a center of learning, and the enormously important and exciting message about it which they were designed to convey. For one thing, where is that liquid simplicity? Where, so often, is impeccable taste and judgment? You know the answer as well as I do: they come with a shock of recognition in the rare and unusual communication at low pressure. [2]

Mr. McCord laments the fact that in the alumni secretaries' continual effort to enlist the continuing support of the graduates of our institutions of higher education, "we are somehow failing to communicate with them in the language and with the dignity and distinctive grace which, among other things, their money is given to uphold." He sums up his burden of complaint in two sentences: "Let me repeat in other words: it is our function to make friends and to strengthen friendly ties. Our dollar return should be predicated on that and on that alone." [3]

Everyone concerned with fund-raising for a college or university would be wise to make common cause with Mr. McCord. In college promotional literature, as in letters of request, there is no legitimate place for "hard sell." Neither is there a place for tasteless gimcracks. A few alumni may be impressed by "hard sell" methods, or amused by messages of appeal conceived in cartoons. These alumni, on the whole, are not believed to be representative.

But humor, joined with tact and verbal skill, has its solid place in the language of request. The Ludgin letters are masterful examples of that language. During the recent capital-gifts campaign of the University of Chicago, Mr. Earle Ludgin, of the class of 1920, was alumni national co-chairman. His series of letters to Chicago alumni spanned four years, and undoubtedly had good effect in the university's raising its quota of $33 million. Here is how, in a letter written in 1953 or 1954, Mr. Ludgin deftly touched on the delicate question of how much to give:

. . . How much should you give? There is no answer an outsider can make. I can only remember the story they tell about W. C. Fields when he was testifying in a lawsuit. His habits of sobriety were in question, and he was asked how much he actually drank— for example, was it about a quart a day? "A quart!" said Fields, "why I spill that much!"

Surely you have some spillage too. How much could you spill and not miss, to help the University continue to be the great University it was in your day and mine? Make your check as generous as you can . . .[4]

The Time–Life Award for 1955–1956, in the annual direct mail competition run by the American Alumni Council, was awarded to the University of Chicago in recognition of the Ludgin letters. Some of these and excerpts of others were published in a special brochure by the American Alumni Council (a brochure which belongs in the literature of fund-raising). Here is a typical gem, processed on a beautifully designed but inexpensive letterhead:

October 25, 1955

Dear Fellow Alumnus:

We're looking for a man with a million dollars. Now don't write back that you are, too. That kind of correspondence simply won't get us anywhere.

Of course somebody will suggest that we ought to settle for a hundred men with ten thousand dollars. Or a thousand men with a thousand dollars each. But before we do that let's consider what awaits that lucky chap with the million. We can't have him painted in that group of Michelangelo's familiars in the corner of "The Last Judgment" or have him portrayed in six volumes by James Boswell. But we can offer him a piece of immortality:

We can name a building after him.

Now as you know buildings cost considerably more than a million dollars. The new Law School, for example, will run to three and a half million at least. If a man were a shrewd buyer, even if not a lawyer himself, he couldn't do better than to snap up that building for his own. First of all, it is being designed by Eero Saarinen, the noted architect, who has just completed his first scale model, which indicates a distinguished design with a commanding use of space. It is to be on the south side of the Midway, next to the headquarters of the American Bar Association. Both legal and educational history are sure to be written there.

If our man would prefer a dormitory, for which countless students will bless his name, or a building for one of the sciences, we have those to offer too. But please note: Only one building to a customer at this low rate. Our only reason for making this offer at all is because, as perhaps you know, the first million is always the hardest to get. We anticipate no trouble in finding the minor millions that must follow.

Great things, stupendous things flow from a gift of this consequence. Consider that the atomic motor of the *Nautilus* was made possible by the work of the scientists at the Argonne Laboratory. And the electric power from atomic sources used in Oregon to light a city's streets came from other Argonne plans. Wouldn't you have been proud to give the millions for that great seat of science?

Consider too that what is done at the University is of importance throughout the world of education. A number of the Alumni at the Chancellor's Conference last February, who are members of the boards of state universities, said that the standards established at Chicago *raised* the standards of universities throughout the country. Reluctant legislators have regularly been led to provide funds for state universities by hearing what the University of Chicago has done, and by being urged not to fall behind Chicago as a matter of state pride.

So please look around the house carefully. People keep money in the oddest places. They say that when Bing Crosby's house burned to the ground a few years ago, he was too late to save anything except an old pair of shoes. In them he had tucked $16,000. Would you look in old shoes, hat boxes, tea caddies, aprons, golf trophies, and behind the books? We need that million dollars.

Very sincerely,

(signed)   (signed)

Earle Ludgin   John J. McDonough

National Co-Chairmen

P.S. Be sure to write your name plainly, so we'll spell it right on your building.[5]

Salesmanship in Print

Advertising and promotional material—defined by a practitioner, Claude Hopkins, as "salesmanship in print"—can be a powerful aid to a letter or a personal call. Some publications are merely informational; some are persuasive. Both kinds may be used with good effect, as, for example, by Rensselaer Polytechnic Institute, to keep the total constituency informed. Regular bulletins, copies of key speeches and of pertinent news stories, and special booklets or leaflets all have their uses. So have fact sheets which will fit into looseleaf binders.

College and university printing budgets are nearly always limited, and hence should be expended on the best printing that can be purchased. One distinguished piece of printing will do more to advance a college fund-raising campaign than a dozen that are poorly written, designed, and produced.

For its 1948–1950 development program, Massachusetts Institute of Technology issued an 11″ × 14″ brochure of twenty pages entitled "Engineers Must Be Citizens Too!" It was well designed but not lavish, and made a good case for the $20,287,500 which the institute was seeking to meet specific objectives. (As reported in Chapter V, M.I.T. received $25,668,532 in contributions during that capital-gifts campaign.)

In 1951, on the occasion of its 250th anniversary, Yale University published a brochure of thirty-six pages, also 11" × 14", entitled "Yale Plans for the Future." It set forth the university's plan of development as prepared by the president and fellows, members of the faculty, and alumni committees.*

During 1957 a considerable number of colleges and universities ordered, for use in their annual giving campaigns, copies of "The Closing College Door," the booklet prepared by the Council for Financial Aid to Education for use in the higher education campaign which it sponsored and the Advertising Council of America conducted. This use of the booklet was suggested by the American Alumni Council. The Ohio State University alone ordered 109,000 copies for mailing to alumni and to parents of presently enrolled students. Princeton University posted copies to 41,000 alumni as promotion for its annual giving campaign ending in February 1958, and attached to each copy a tastefully printed "hanger" with a message from President Robert F. Goheen.

The cost of this 5½" × 8½" sixteen-page booklet was 1.8 cents a copy, plus shipping charges. Nearly one million copies have been ordered by American colleges and universities for use in their mail solicitations.

Also widely used, on a bulk order basis, have been a series of leaflets published by the Council for Financial Aid to Education, each one directed to a special aspect of the nature and

* Such is the pace of events and such are the demands on American higher educational institutions that this plan was superseded in 1957 by the $109,745,000 development recommended by the University Council.

needs of American higher education. These have been furnished at cost of production plus postage, and have been used by the colleges as objective arguments for "the case bigger than the institution."

These colleges and universities know, and all others should perceive, that their constituents must be kept informed—but not saturated—by the printed as well as the spoken word of request.

How to Conduct Mail Appeals

In the actual carrying out of a solicitation by mail, probably no college or group of colleges has had sounder experience than the United Negro College Fund. This experience has been distilled into guidance notes for the fund's local committees all over the nation.[6]

First of all, the UNCF states what has been proved thoroughly: "There is no equally effective substitute for personal solicitation," and adds that the annual campaign is little likely to reach its goal unless the chairman and his associates "deal personally with a reasonable number of important prospects."

An appeal by mail usually nets a low percentage of participation. It does well to get 60 per cent of former contributors to repeat. As for non-givers, a 3 or 4 per cent response is the most to be expected. For these reasons and because mail appeals seldom seek proportionate giving, the response to mail appeals in dollar volume is usually low.

Also, the percentage cost of raising money by mail is seldom less than 25 or 30 per cent. Often it runs higher. In contrast, organized appeals based mainly on personal solicitation seldom have costs exceeding 15 per cent, and may go much lower than this.

The attention-getting strength of the appeal generally depends on the degree to which the appeal appears to be personal and individual. It is a waste of time and money to send a mimeographed letter with the "Dear Friend" salutation and a rubber stamp signature.

People are most likely to contribute if asked to do so by some person with whom they are frequently in direct contact in their business or social life.

Successful appeals by mail must have repetition and continuity, and so should provide for one or more follow-up letters. Especially with previous non-givers, it is more fruitful to write to one good prospect three times than to appeal only once to three times as long a list.

Habit patterns greatly influence contributing by mail. Once a giver starts giving a certain amount, at a certain season of the year, only personal solicitation is likely to raise his level of giving. So it is well, in addressing new prospects, to strive at the outset for some reasonable measure of proportionate giving.

Moving from principles to procedures, the UNCF suggests first of all determining the constituency to be approached, and then who will sign the mail appeals. The fund suggests it is well to keep in mind that the effectiveness of the sponsorship will be in direct proportion to the writer's frequency of normal contact with the prospects who are to be solicited.

Great care has to be taken in planning the mechanics of the mailing—the nature and quantity of essential envelopes, letterheads, leaflets, and subscription forms, and how the appeal letter is to be processed. The size and weight of enclosures must be kept in mind. Any good lettershop can explain the various methods by which letters are processed and by which they can be hand-signed.

Especially when the list includes not more than two-hundred names, letters to large contributors and important prospects are sometimes auto-typed—written on electric typewriters which are first guided through a full three- or four-line salutation and then complete the common body of the letter, working from an impressed cylinder. Such letters even permit inclusion of sentences directed to each individual, such as mention of what he has given in previous years. In appearance these letters are the equal of individually typed communications.

It is important to set the timing of the appeal, not merely for the original letter but for any follow-ups. Generally, letters timed to arrive in mid-week are the most effective.

Also it is important to estimate the cost of the entire mailing, so that the plan can cover all necessary requirements and still be kept within reasonable bounds.

Mail appeals nearly always need a leaflet enclosure to dramatize the argument through pictures or printed text, and usually to give additional information that will help to stir into action the impulse to give. But it is wise to avoid too many enclosures.

On suggestions for writing the appeal letter the United Negro College Fund is especially clear:

Anyone preparing copy for letters seeking to raise money by mail would do well to study the copy and techniques employed by the subscription departments of important national magazines, or by commercial organizations which successfully sell by mail.

Raising money by mail is even more difficult, as the only direct reward to the donor is personal satisfaction. Appeal letters, therefore, should pay thoughful attention to four basic essentials:

Personalize
Dramatize
Popularize
Particularize

The UNCF advises that especially careful thought be given to the first line of the letter, and to the close. The lead should entice the reader in, and the ending should give him a clear indication of what he is being asked to do, and when.

The use of an addressed reply envelope increases the percentage of response. Many donors dislike having to affix postage stamps to return envelopes.

Summary

All that a college or university can muster of skill, taste, and intelligence is needed to cultivate its total constituency, the "fit though few."

Any letter or publication sent by a college in a mail solicitation should represent the institution's personality or "tone."

A college should take pains to speak in "the language of request." Alumni secretaries and all others who seek money for a college or university should speak and act as "an extension of, and not simply a blunt instrument for, our alma mater." [7]

The leaven of humor, along with tact and dignity, has its place in the language of request.

Promotional material can of course be a powerful aid to a letter or a personal call.

One distinguished piece of printing will do more to advance a college fund-raising campaign than a dozen that are poorly written, designed, and produced.

A college's constituents must be kept informed—but not saturated—by means of the printed as well as the spoken word of request.

A mail solicitation is usually a low producer of gifts. However, principles and procedures like those worked out by the United Negro College Fund will help to make it as effective as possible.

REFERENCES

Chapter XIII

1. David McCord, "The Language of Request," *American Alumni Council News,* April 1957, pp. 8–10. The whole article is recommended reading for anyone concerned with college fund-raising.

2. *Ibid.,* p. 9.
3. *Ibid.,* pp. 9, 10.
4. *The 1955–1956 Time-Life Award-Winning Direct Mail Letters of the University of Chicago.* (Washington, D.C.: The American Alumni Council, November 1, 1956), p. 20. Credit and thanks are given to Earle Ludgin and the University of Chicago campaign.
5. *Ibid.,* pp. 6–7.
6. The United Negro College Fund's mimeograph, "How to Conduct a Mail Appeal," has been used with the permission of the fund. Some of the principles and procedures were suggested to it by Mr. Harold J. Seymour.
7. David McCord, *op. cit.,* p. 10.

XIV   Tax Benefits to Donors

"It was as true," said Mr. Barkis, ". . . as
taxes is. And nothing's truer than them."

—DICKENS, *David Copperfield*

The Internal Revenue Code, effective in 1936, has become
more relaxed with regard to voluntary giving for charitable,
educational, and religious causes—by business corporations as
well as individuals. The effect of the code, further revised in
1954, is to make the Federal Government a partner in voluntary giving.

Many colleges and universities have issued publications in-
forming their constituencies about tax benefits as related to
personal or corporation giving. Amherst College in 1953 issued an excellent guide, "Tax Aspects of a Gift to Amherst,"
and revised it in 1954. Dartmouth College published a similar
guide (referred to in Chapter IX of this book) in 1951, and
revised it in 1952 and again in 1953. Also, the J. K. Lasser
Tax Institute annually brings out a new edition of its sixteen-
page, 4" × 9" "Contributor's Income Tax Deduction Guide,"
which any charitable, educational, or religious institution can
use to advantage for promotional purposes.

Some Provisions of the Internal Revenue Code

As everybody connected with college fund-raising should
know, a principal effect of the Internal Revenue Code is to
make the Federal Government the chief contributor of gifts to
educational and charitable institutions which individuals in the
high income brackets make to them. If he takes the maximum

in tax benefits, an individual with an adjusted gross income of $500,000 or more can make a $1,000 gift to his college at a net cost of $90. The Federal exemption on this gift would be $910, so the central government would be a 91 per cent partner in it. Numerous states have passed statutes giving similar tax benefits to residents; so if the giver just cited were resident in one of these states, the ultimate cost to him of the $1,000 gift would be still lower.

Amherst gives illustrations of how the cost of a gift to the college is reduced by the Federal income tax deduction:

For married men with taxable net incomes over $12,000, the net cost of a gift to the College is less than three-fourths of the amount given.

For those with incomes over $42,000 it is less than half.

For those with net incomes over $140,000 it is less than one-fourth.*

In effect, the donor's gift reduces the amount of his income to be taxed; he saves the tax on the income equal to the amount of his gift. And the higher his income, the larger the saving, since the gift deduction shaves off the top level of his income in his highest tax bracket.

Under 1954 I.R.C. rates, the real net cost at varying income levels of gifts by a man with two children to a college or university, appears in the following table:

---

* The figures given in this paragraph are high enough to allow a gift at the cost indicated, up to the maximum allowable 30 per cent of adjusted gross income. For small gifts the proportion of net cost indicated will be applicable to lower taxable net incomes. Tax rates from the 1954 Internal Revenue Code are used in all examples. These figures refer to net income after the personal exemption and dependency credits are taken.

Adjusted Gross Income	Net Cost of First $1,000 of Gift	Percentage of First $1,000 Borne by Government	Maximum Deductible Gift	Net Cost of Maximum Deductible Gift
$ 5,000	$800	20	$ 1,500	$ 1,200
6,000	800	20	1,800	1,440
7,000	800	20	2,100	1,680
8,000	784	21.6	2,400	1,904
9,000	780	22	2,700	2,126
10,000	780	22	3,000	2,348
15,000	740	26	4,500	3,386
20,000	700	30	6,000	4,296
25,000	656	34.4	7,500	5,082
30,000	590	41	9,000	5,742
35,000	530	47	10,500	6,267
40,000	500	50	12,000	6,688
50,000	440	56	15,000	7,372
75,000	350	65	22,500	8,841
100,000	310	69	30,000	10,228
200,000	160	84	60,000	11,616
300,000	110	89	90,000	10,420
500,000	90	91	150,000	14,548

This table is based on married taxpayer, two children, other (non-charitable) deductions of 10 per cent of adjusted gross income.

As illustrated in column four of the table above, a contributor to an established educational institution is permitted to deduct the full amount of his gifts up to 30 per cent of his adjusted gross income for Federal income tax purposes. Also, most states which have income tax laws grant comparable deductions. There is no Federal gift tax on a donor's contributions made during his lifetime. Gifts by will, moreover, are deductible for Federal or state estate or inheritance tax purposes.

A business corporation may deduct its contributions up to 5 per cent of its net income in computing its corporate income tax liability. (In 1954, the last year on which the Internal Revenue Service has to date reported on the statistics of income, the average rate for some 722,000 companies was .84 of 1 per cent.)

As is explained in "Tax Aspects of a Gift to Amherst":

The effect of these special allowances is to make the Federal government and in some cases your state government joint contributors to every educational gift you make. The policy is designed to give private citizens an extra incentive to shoulder an educational burden which might otherwise fall entirely upon the government.

Ways in Which Contributions Can Be Made

Some of the methods of giving, with tax benefits, to a college or university have been described in Chapter IX, on estate planning. They will simply be listed here, as a reminder, along with other methods of making gifts to colleges and universities:

By money, check.

In the form of household property—as, for example, books, paintings, other art objects.

In the form of business property.

In the form of other property such as real estate, life insurance, annuities, and securities.

Mailing a contribution check has been ruled to be the same as giving it to the college or university. A donor who posts a check on December 31 can deduct it in computing his income tax for the year ending then, even though the institution receives it in the following year.

A GIFT OF PROPERTY

A gift of property is equally deductible; the amount of the deduction is the value of the property. One result of a gift of property is to increase the donor's "spendable" cash.

For example, a retired alumnus with a net income of $10,-000 gives accumulated property worth $3,000 to his college.

Taking this deduction, he reduces his Federal income tax to
$1,560, and gains $860 in cash. If he had not made the gift
his tax would have been $2,420.*

Gifts of property may offer another advantage over gifts
made in cash. If you give property which has increased in
value since you acquired it, you may deduct its market value.
The appreciation in value is not taxed to you as a gain. So the
real cost of the gift to the donor is further reduced. For if he
should sell the appreciated property instead of giving it to X
college, it would net him not its sale price but only its sale
price minus the capital gains tax he would have to pay on the
sale.

Amherst gives the example of an alumnus whose net income
is $20,000. He gives to the college securities worth $4,000.
More than six months previously they cost him $2,000. If he
sells the securities he will keep only $3,500—the selling price
less $500, the 25 per cent tax on the $2,000 gain. His income
tax at present rates is $4,560 with benefit of the deduction for
the gift. Without the deduction, his tax would have been
$6,260. The gift saves the donor $1,700 in taxes, so its net
cost to him is $3,500 less $1,700, or $1,800. At the same time
the college holds securities upon which it can immediately
realize $4,000 in cash.

In the event property has increased greatly in value and the
donor is in a high tax bracket, the results of the gift of the
property to a college are startling. As an example, a donor has
net income of $100,000 and a piece of property which cost
him $2,000 but is now worth $20,000. If he sells the property
he will receive $20,000, but pay a capital gains tax of $4,500.
He will net $15,500. If he gives the property to his college his

* In this and the next two examples it has been assumed that the
donor files his tax return as an unmarried man who is "head of a
household." If the donor is unmarried and not "head of a household"
or is married, the results will be somewhat different.

deduction will save him $15,600 in taxes. The donor actually can do better financially by giving the property to the college than by selling it.

On the other hand, a donor should not ordinarily give property which has declined in value. He does better to sell the property in order to gain the tax benefit of the loss, and contribute the proceeds of the sale. If the property is a personal asset (a sculpture, an automobile) the donor cannot get a tax loss on the sale. He gains only by giving it directly to the college of his choice.

COST OF TESTAMENTARY GIFTS TO A COLLEGE

Educational bequests are deductible without limitation in computing a person's taxable estate; hence he can make testamentary gifts to a college with little diminution of the portion of his estate remaining for other purposes. This is particularly true if the estate is large.

The following table shows the net diminution per $1,000 of bequests to a college or university from estates of varying sizes, after the Federal estate tax:

Net Estate Before Bequests *	Net Diminution per $1,000 Bequest	Percentage of Bequest Borne by Government
$ 100,000	$720	28
250,000	700	30
500,000	680	32
1,000,000	630	37
1,500,000	580	42
2,000,000	550	45
5,000,000	370	63
10,000,000	240	76
20,000,000	230	77

* After all deductions, including the marital deduction and the $60,000 general exemption. For example, a net estate of $260,000 before the marital deduction and the general exemption becomes a net estate of $100,000 after those allowances are subtracted.

In most states an individual's estate will also be subject to state estate or inheritance taxes. The Federal estate tax law allows a limited credit for these taxes against the federal estate impost. These state taxes, however, may exceed this credit. If they do, the individual's testamentary gifts to a college will probably cause even less reduction of his remaining estate, since he will save on state succession taxes.

One fact not widely enough realized is that an individual can, through giving to a college or university, eliminate Federal estate tax liability altogether. If a man or woman leaves his entire estate to a college or university of his choice, there will of course be no Federal estate tax at all. The individual may also avoid incurring any estate tax whatever by taking advantage of the general deduction of $60,000 and the marital deduction to husband or wife not exceeding one-half of the estate. In this way it is possible to leave one-half of one's estate to one's spouse, $60,000 in any way one chooses, and the rest to a college or university—and incur no Federal estate tax.

The chief disadvantage of making educational gifts by will rather than during an individual's lifetime is that he loses the valuable income tax deduction annually. Lifetime educational gifts indirectly afford the same estate tax advantage as testamentary gifts; the deducted property is simply not on hand to be included in the taxable estate.

In a word, careful selection of the time and manner of giving to a college or university may produce maximum tax savings, as the Federal Government urges taxpayers to do; and in some cases it may produce collateral benefits useful in managing the donor's affairs and in planning his estate.[1]

Summary

The Internal Revenue Code makes the Federal Government a partner in individual philanthropy. But the tax savings are greatest for individuals in the highest income brackets.

If he gives to educational, health, or religious organizations, the individual taxpayer is entitled to deduct up to 30 per cent of his adjusted gross income for Federal income tax purposes.

Most states which have income tax laws grant comparable deductions. Donors may contribute to colleges and universities in various ways: by money or check, in the form of personal or household property, in the form of business property, and in the form of other property such as real estate, life insurance, annuities, and securities.

There are advantages in lifetime giving which are lost in testamentary giving.

Careful selection of the time and manner of giving to a college or university may produce maximum tax savings. In some cases, careful selection may produce collateral benefits useful in managing the donor's affairs and in planning his estate.

REFERENCE

Chapter XIV

1. Generous reference has been made throughout this chapter to "Tax Aspects of a Gift to Amherst," with the full permission of the college. The booklet was written by the late Randolph Paul, Amherst 1911, a leading tax authority. In its field it is unsurpassed.

XV   A Working Program

> Burrow a while and build, broad on the
> roots of things.
>
> —BROWNING, *Abt Vogler*

Any college that wishes to keep its household affairs in good order must seek adequate financial support on a regular, continuous basis from all of its "identifiable constituencies." The president of a Pennsylvania college went to the heart of the matter when he said, "I have little patience with those institutions which are waiting around piteously for someone to help them out of their troubles. We are doing more things for ourselves—with our alumni, with our church connections, with our budget-making and budget-control, with our policy on tuition and fees." At the same time he welcomed aid from industry as a means of doing not merely a good but a first class job.

Any college which is doing a good job in an area where it needs to be done can organize a development program. Best results may be obtained if at least one full time staff member is in charge of it. On the other hand, in a small college operating on a tight budget the program could, *with active trustee participation,* be managed at the outset by a member of the administration or faculty. After growth it should be turned over to a person giving his full time to the job.

To the objection "We can't afford to have a development program" the answer is "You can't raise money without spending money, and without adequate funds you can't live." A survey conducted during 1957 by the Council for Financial

Aid to Education * showed that an encouraging number of the nation's colleges, universities, and professional schools now conduct development programs. Many are in charge of full time directors.

Four essentials of a working program for college development warrant re-emphasis here:

1. An active trustees' committee on finance and development is a first requisite. (In Catholic colleges, this role can be filled by the governing order, or by a lay committee in co-operation with it.)

2. The program must have constant direction and service from the college or university itself.

3. There must be a reliable and committed corps of volunteers to make the various committees function well.

4. The development program, which is indispensable, is built on hard, intelligent work.

A Co-ordinated Plan

The business of the development council is to plan and co-ordinate the total fund-raising of the college or university. By its existence the council insures against the very real danger that individual fund-raising projects fostered by enthusiastic groups of the constituency will come into conflict and thus threaten the success of the over-all movement. It is of the utmost importance that the council develop a comprehensive plan of development based on careful analysis of the situation at hand, and harmoniously fuse all of the different activities involved in the plan. Better relations with the constituency inevitably result; likewise, better financial returns to the institution.

It is wise practice for the chairman of the development council to designate five or six of its members to constitute a

* In co-operation with the American Alumni Council and the American College Public Relations Association.

subcommittee on planning which will study, correlate, and interpret to the council the foreseeable needs of the college or university during the period of ten to twenty-five years immediately ahead. This subcommittee would be expected to keep the council aware of the probable needs of the institution as soon as they can be foreseen. Two services can be performed by such a subcommittee. It can keep in view a comprehensive picture of the institution's future needs. It can thus make it possible to present these needs well in advance in order to bring them to the attention of prospects, on the lists of the development council, who might be induced to help meet these needs either by gifts or by bequests. It is important that the college or university know in good season what its needs will be.

A useful tool for the council is a looseleaf binder containing a list of these needs, the various ways of giving to the college or university, and information about its accomplishments, its graduates, and the trustees. Stanford University uses with excellent effect what it calls the "R-book," initialed for the man who conceived the idea of it or compiled the information that was put into it. The book gives a clear and convincing exposition of Stanford's *case*. It also has the virtue of being current. From time to time the Stanford Fund (development council) brings certain parts or pages of the book up to date and sends them, for substitution, to fund members and other persons possessing copies. "Other persons" include a considerable number of lawyers and trust officers in the "Stanford family."

Knox College and Union College (Schenectady) are among other institutions that have issued similar books. They represent a fruitful investment.

Operating Schedule

An annual meeting of the development council should be held on the campus. The purpose would be to review the progress of the council's work in the preceding year, and to consider plans and proposals for work in the months ahead. October or June, according to local circumstances, would probably be the best time for this meeting.

The director of development should prepare an annual report for this meeting, addressed to the chairman of the council. In turn the report should be relayed to the board of trustees.

Beyond this, the director of development should prepare a quarterly report. This should be sent to all members of the development council. It should outline plans for their consideration and review the progress of the council's fund-raising activities.

Although responsible to the Board of Trustees, the director of development should confer at a stated weekly time (so far as possible) with the president and such other members of the steering committee as are on the campus. The chairman of this committee, and also the chairman of the trustees' committee on finance and development (if they are not the same person), should be strongly urged to attend these meetings at least once a month if possible.

The director of the Alumni Fund should be invited to attend these meetings regularly. Whether or not he belonged to the committee would have to be determined by local considerations.

There should be no conflict between the activities of the development council and those of the annual alumni fund. All alumni, regardless of whether or not their names are in the files of the council, should be invited to contribute to the "living endowment" program every year. This program is a continuous one which should give the institution's alumni an opportunity to contribute to the immediate operating needs and to match their loyalty against that of other colleges and universities. The gifts secured by the development council are mainly capital gifts. These preferably should not be counted in the totals and class percentages shown in the alumni fund reports. While the capital gifts secured by the development council will in many instances come from alumni, they will be obtained only from alumni who are well able to participate with the other members of their classes in the annual "loyalty round-up." Both undertakings will encourage the giving habit among the alumni and thus should be mutually helpful.

While the alumni secretary should be kept fully informed of the development council's program, he personally should have no responsibility for it beyond giving it his enthusiastic moral support and furnishing advice and suggestions concerning alumni who in his judgment should qualify as special gift or bequest prospects.

Individual conferences with members of the development council are indispensable. At least once a year the director of development and/or the chairman of the council should visit each of its members in his home city to confer with him and any other local persons he may select. This visit would keep the council member up to date on the council's program, stimulate his thinking and action, and make possible an on-the-spot appraisal of opportunities for special gifts, bequests, or corporation gifts. Also it would establish the most opportune time or times for officers of the college or university, including the president, to visit the city in question for personal calls on prospects.

In addition, the president, alumni secretary, or director of development should visit each alumni club throughout the country at least once a year, not to solicit funds but to bring the alumni a first-hand report designed to maintain their lively interest in the institution.

Headquarters Activities

The names of the persons and companies with whom the list committee of the development council will be concerned should include only those who in the past have contributed $500 or more to the institution, and also those who, in the judgment of the council, are able and may be willing to make such gifts. These prospective givers will fall into three categories: 1) alumni special donors and prospective alumni special donors, 2) individual non-alumni special donors and prospective non-alumni special donors, and 3) business concerns which are special donors or prospective special donors.

The names in these three categories should be recorded on cards of three different colors. A separate file should be kept for each group, and in turn each group should be divided into two sections, one for those who have given or are giving and the other for those who are able to and may give. A duplicate set of all of these cards should be made so that a complete alphabetical file and a complete geographical file will be available.

Since it is unlikely that the original list will be large, it should not be difficult to maintain these duplicate files. And the advantages to be derived from having this information available both alphabetically and geographically will far outweigh the trouble it takes to keep up the duplicate files.

A note of emphasis and a word of caution are in order here. Where the personal touch can be applied, it will do the most to cultivate potential givers. Every effort should thus be made to see what person in the constituency can most effectively approach each listed prospect. And that should be only the first fact ascertained. Each prospect listed should be carefully "researched" before he is assigned to the most effective possible solicitor, and these further facts should be discovered: solid evidence of ability to give, interest in higher education, record of gifts to it, things of special interest to the individual or company (such as art, drama, literature, medicine, music, or science), and any other information that would help the development council to know the prospect.

It is suggested that the geographical file be tabbed to indicate the special interests of each prospect listed, so that announcements of events of interest in his special fields may be sent to him. Announcements or invitations to concerts or lectures should be sent even to persons located at a distance from the institution, simply to keep them informed and interested, and regardless of whether or not it is likely they could attend. Consideration might be given to the maintenance of addressograph plates for use in sending out such announcements and invitations.

Prospect Cultivation

It should be the policy of the development council and college or university officials to cultivate each special donor and each prospective special donor as if he were the one person in whom the institution is especially interested. Moreover, every opportunity should be seized to express to him the institution's thanks and appreciation for his gifts, or for any other expressions of his friendliness.

Occasions should be developed to enable the president of the institution or some member of the development council to invite as many as possible of the listed special donors or prospective special donors to visit the campus at least once a year. The occasions should be staggered so that the officers of the institution can give these special visitors personal attention and thus develop their interest in it.

The director of development should see to it that the president has grounds to write a personal letter at least once a year to every special donor and prospective special donor on the list. He should also be responsible for seeing that these letters are written and mailed.

If he is not already receiving it, each person on the development council's cultivation list should be sent the institution's alumni magazine. He should also receive commencement invitations and announcements concerning special events which may be of interest to him. In addition, he should receive any special bulletins pertaining to the institution's work and needs which may be published.

All of the work of cultivation so far mentioned can readily be organized or controlled from development council headquarters. Reaching isolated prospects for gifts is less easy, but the development council can resort to four methods: 1) delegating the responsibility to the committee member nearest the prospect, and asking him to undertake to secure a gift, 2) having the president or some other officer of the institution or a member of the development council make a special trip to see him personally, 3) having the president or some other officer or a member of the council join forces with one or more alumni in the city concerned to approach the prospect, or 4) sending the prospect a personal letter signed by the president.

In addition to the development council's subcommittee on planning which has already been mentioned, the council should have carefully selected committees on lists, alumni fund, estate planning, foundations, corporations, parents, and any others considered necessary. It is more important that the personnel selected be choice than numerous. The various committees will naturally have to meet a number of times during the year, apart from the annual meeting of the entire development council. The director of development should give the utmost service from headquarters to these committees. They give free time, out of a deep interest, to the development of the college or university. Nothing makes this interest flag so much as poor co-operation or service from development council headquarters.

The task and the *modus operandi* of the committees on alumni fund, estate planning, foundations, and corporations have been indicated in Chapters V, IX, X, and XI, respectively. Suggestions for the list committee have been given earlier in this chapter, and suggestions for the work of the parents committee are contained in Chapter VIII. Here it may be added that it is generally best to have the parents committee separate from the alumni fund, and to have the parents do the asking among their own ranks.

One ultimate responsibility rests upon the director of development—seeing to it that all gifts received through the development council are promptly and gratefully acknowledged. Tastefully printed forms, with room for fill-ins, may be used in many instances. Some colleges and universities, however, acknowledge every gift by letter. In some instances the president may sign; in certain others, the treasurer or another officer. But no matter who, if anybody, signs the acknowledgment or what its form, the director of development must create a system to insure that this indispensable job is done unfailingly.

Summary

When a well managed college or university has important work to do which will advance its growth and development, able and interested people can be enlisted. The work needs to be organized and managed at the institution by a regular member of its staff. Outside counsel may, and in particular cases of record does, help to bring operations to their peak in effectiveness.

The basic fact is, simply, that a development program is an organic part of any institution which aims to grow in quality and in the scope of service provided for its supporting publics. It is important for every college and university and professional school to start a development fund, if one is not already functioning. Then the raising of funds—which are its lifeblood—can be carried on systematically by the institution in good times and bad, in peace and in war, to meet foreseeable needs and to cope with emergencies when they arise.

Index